The Joy of Sisterhood

By
Luerine Madison Spencer

The Joy Of Sisterhood

Published by Creation Publishing Group LLC
www.creationpublishing.com

© 2023 Luerine Madison Spencer
ISBN # 979-8-9857286-3-7

Library of Congress Number # 2023908644

Published and printed in the United States of America.

Acknowledgments

First, I would like to give glory and honor to God for the inspiration to create this book and for giving me my gift of creativity that allows me to share my art with others. Without God, this book would have never come together.

I'd also like to acknowledge and thank Marc Guerrero for helping me with the line drawings to make my dolls ready for coloring. He did a wonderful job converting my color pictures into black and white images so people would have the opportunity to choose their own color schemes to express their creativity.

My son Vann Spencer handled most of the graphic designs and without his patience and dedication this book would have never come to fruition. He is an amazing graphic designer who definitely knows how to express his creativity.

Although she isn't my sister by blood, my friend Ora Hall is a part of my sisterhood and deserves recognition for her insights and contributions towards this project. Her input was invaluable as I put this book together.

I have to give special thanks to my son in law Michael Taylor for sharing his expertise in publishing and for putting together this project. He did a wonderful job putting together all of the pieces to complete this project and then making sure it was published.

Marshall Petway was also instrumental in bringing this book together and I am extremely grateful for his contribution towards this project.

Luerine Madison Spencer

And last but not least, I'd like to thank my grandson, Van Juan Spencer for his expert photography skills and the wonderful job he did photographing my dolls and making them look great.

Of course I'd be remiss if I didn't thank you, the reader, for purchasing this book. Thank you from the bottom of my heart for giving me the opportunity to share my art with you.

Introduction

Growing up with seven sisters was an experience like no other. We were a tight-knit group, each with our own unique personalities and quirks. From the youngest to the eldest, we laughed, fought, cried, and shared countless memories together. As I reflect on those years, I realize that having so many sisters taught me a great deal about the power and joy of sisterhood. Sisterhood is a bond that cannot be broken, and it can bring tremendous happiness and support into our lives. Whether you have one sister or ten, the love and connection that comes with sisterhood can enrich your life in countless ways.

This coloring book is a tribute to sisterhood and my seven sisters. Each of us were blessed with unique gifts and talents and I wanted to showcase them with the illustrations in this book.

So, whether you are a sister yourself or simply curious about the joys of sisterhood, I invite you to join me on this journey of exploring the incredible power of sisterly love.

As black women, it's important for us to have positive role models who can inspire us to reach our full potential and encourage us to discover and express our gifts with the world, so as you're going through this coloring book, I'd like you to recognize that you too have unique gifts and talents and it is your responsibility to discover them and share them with the world.

I come from a large family of sixteen children, eight boys and eight girls. My parents, Charlie and Mary Lee Madison, instilled in us the importance of having a relationship with God, getting a good education, and taking care of your family. We were raised on a farm in Monroeville Alabama and that taught us to have a very strong work ethic, and although we weren't

Luerine Madison Spencer

wealthy, we were rich in the things that mattered most. Things like, love of family, compassion for others, and being active in the community.

If I had to sum up the greatest gift I've been given, it would have to be creativity. Creativity runs throughout my family. I have it, my sisters have it, and my children all have it. As a former art teacher, I was able to not only share my creativity, but I was able to teach my students how to access their creativity.

The dolls you see throughout this book are actually made from toilet paper rolls and fabric which I created myself. These dolls are simply my way of sharing my creativity and my love for my sisters. I love my sisters and I love my creativity.

Thank you for giving me the opportunity to share my creativity with you by purchasing this coloring book. It is a labor of love that I hope will provide you with an opportunity to express your creativity. So be sure to remember what the good book says in Matthew 18:2-4 "Truly I tell you, unless you change and become as little children, you will never enter the kingdom of heaven".

So, grab your crayons or markers and become as little children and have fun expressing your creativity so that you too, can enter the kingdom of heaven.

Luerine Madison Spencer

The Joy of Sisterhood

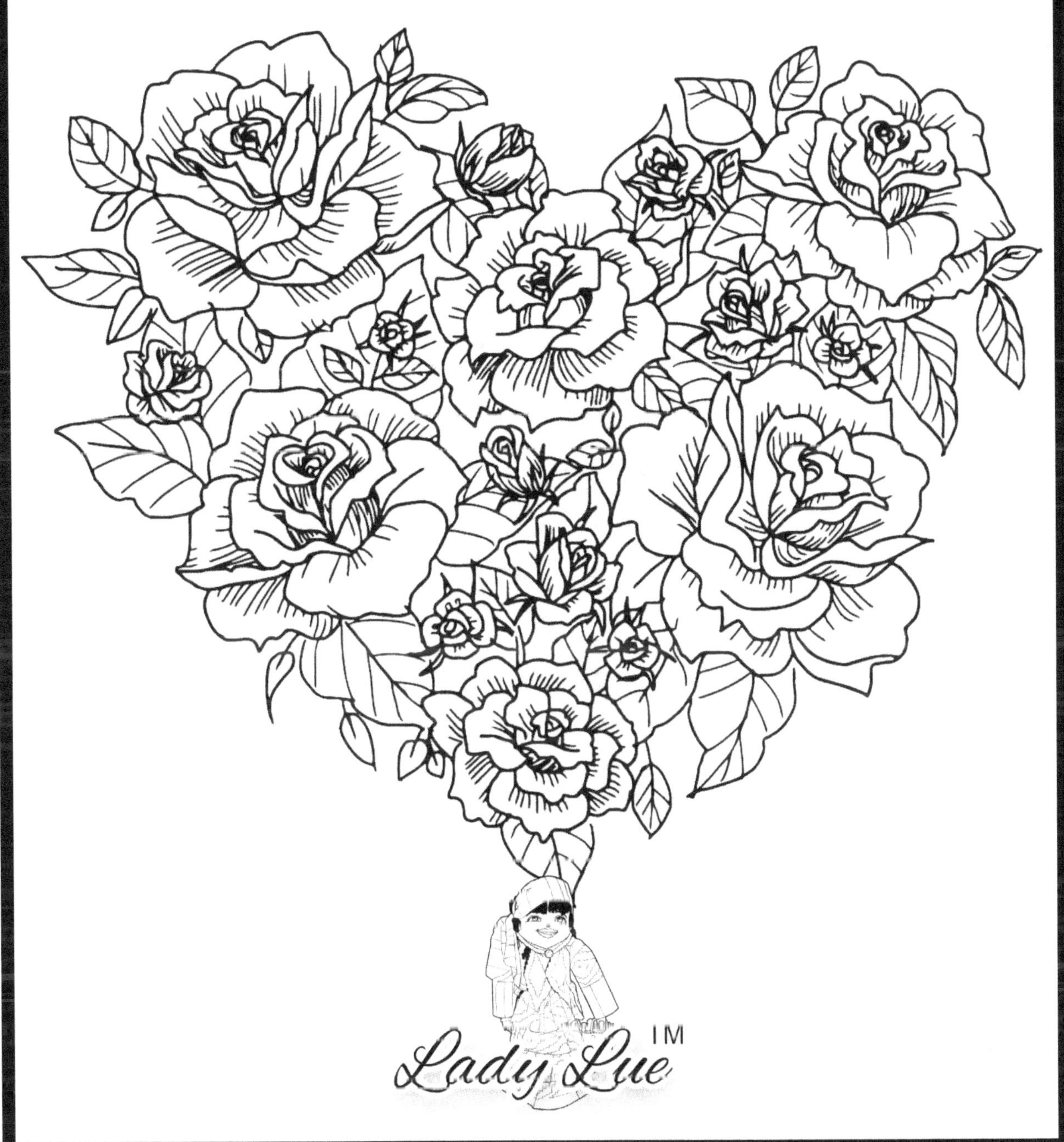

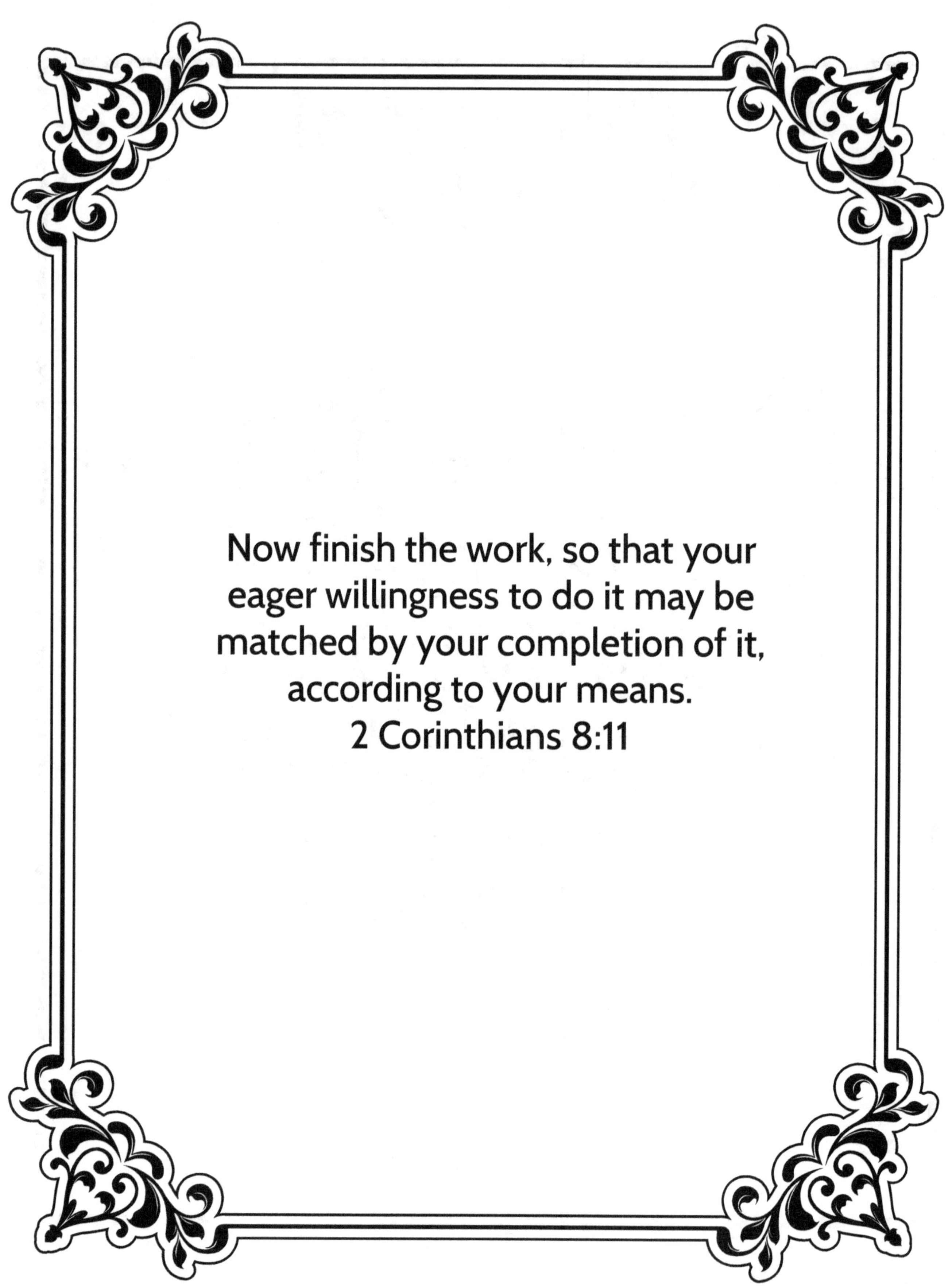

Now finish the work, so that your
eager willingness to do it may be
matched by your completion of it,
according to your means.
2 Corinthians 8:11

1 2 3 4 5 6 7 8 9 10 11 12

13 14 15 16 17 18 19 20 21 22

a b c d e f g h i j k

l m n o p q r s t u v w x y z

Luerine Madison Spencer

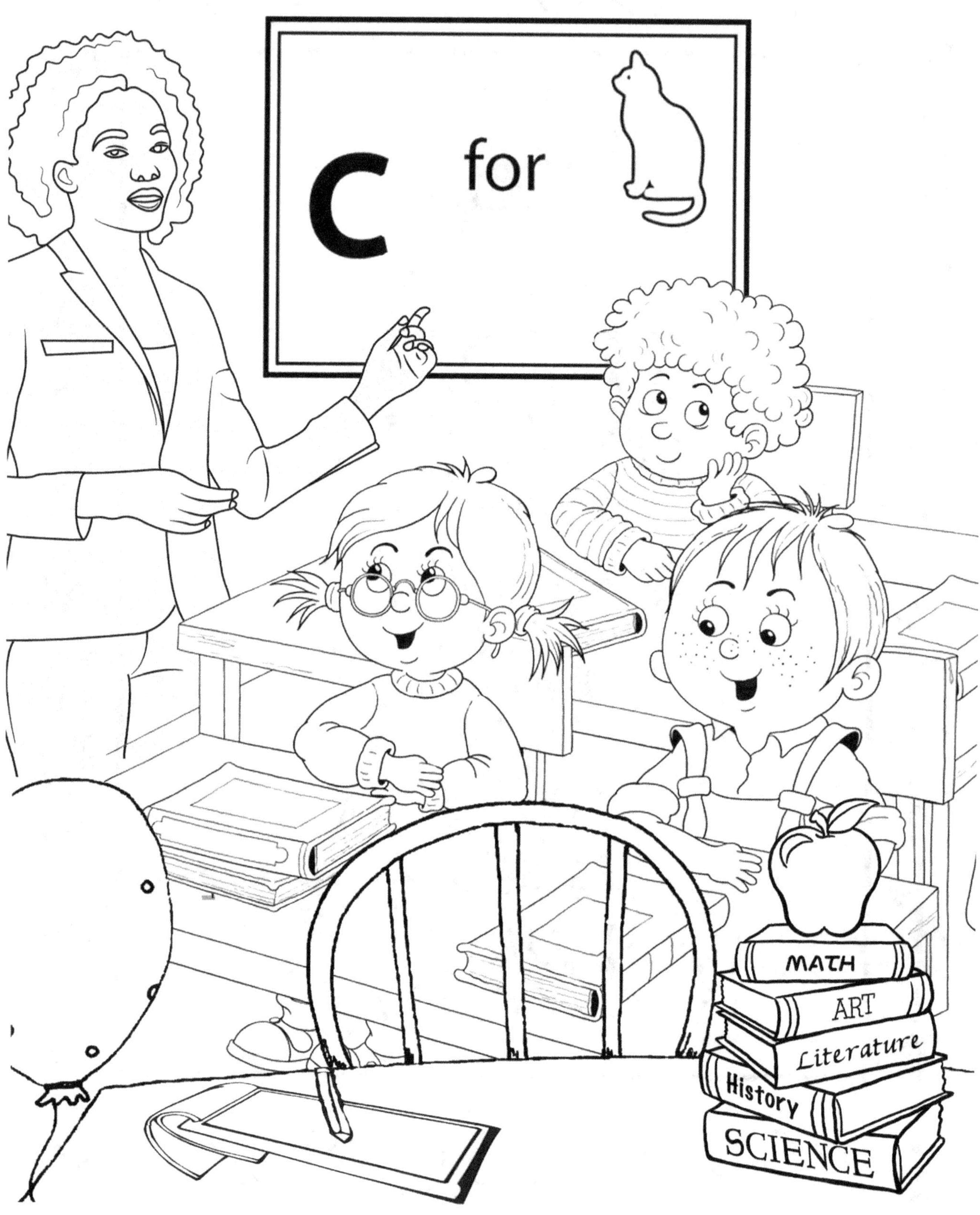

Mary was a Teacher and Chef.
She was the oldest of all
sixteen children

Luerine Madison Spencer

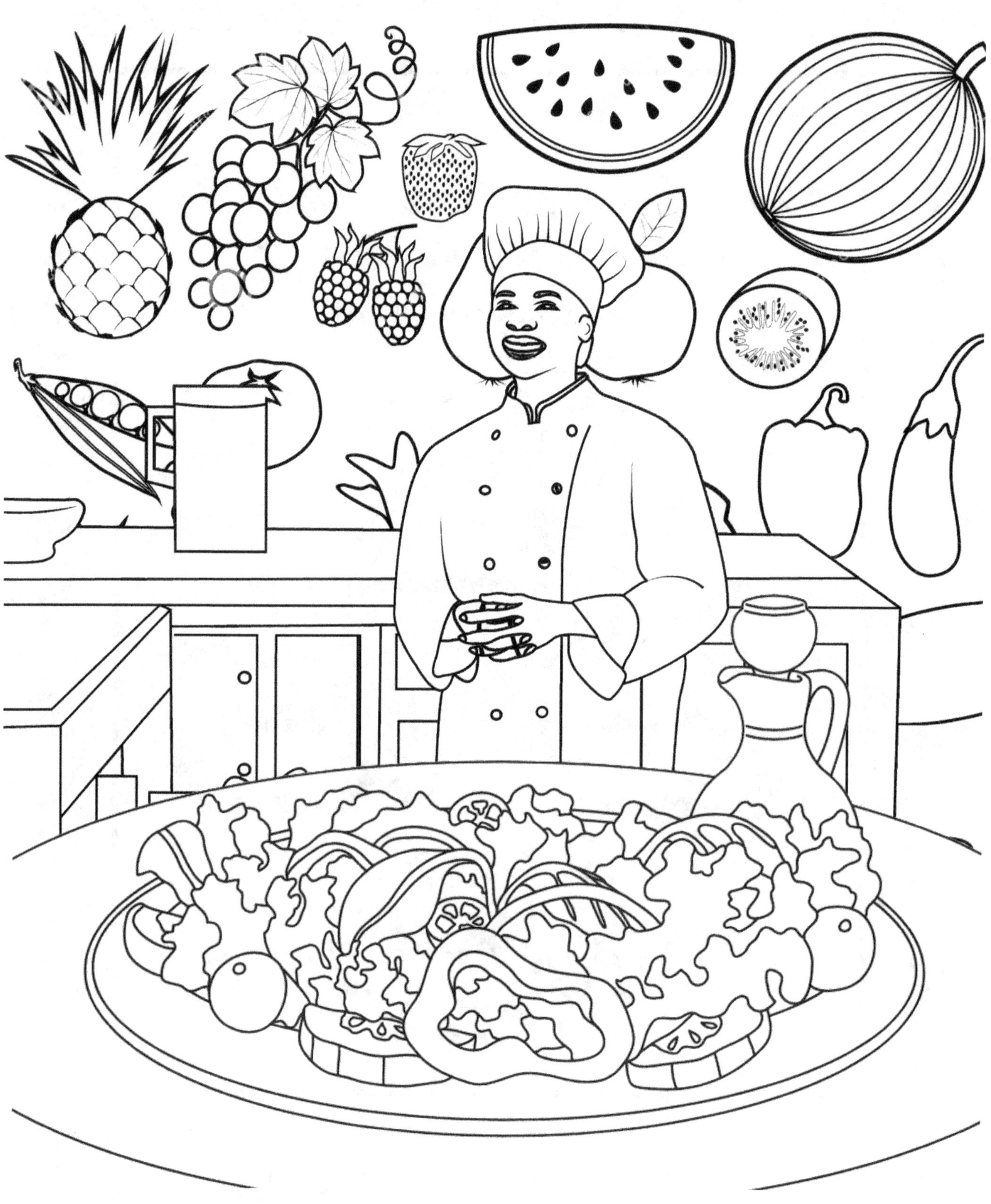

Chef

Teacher

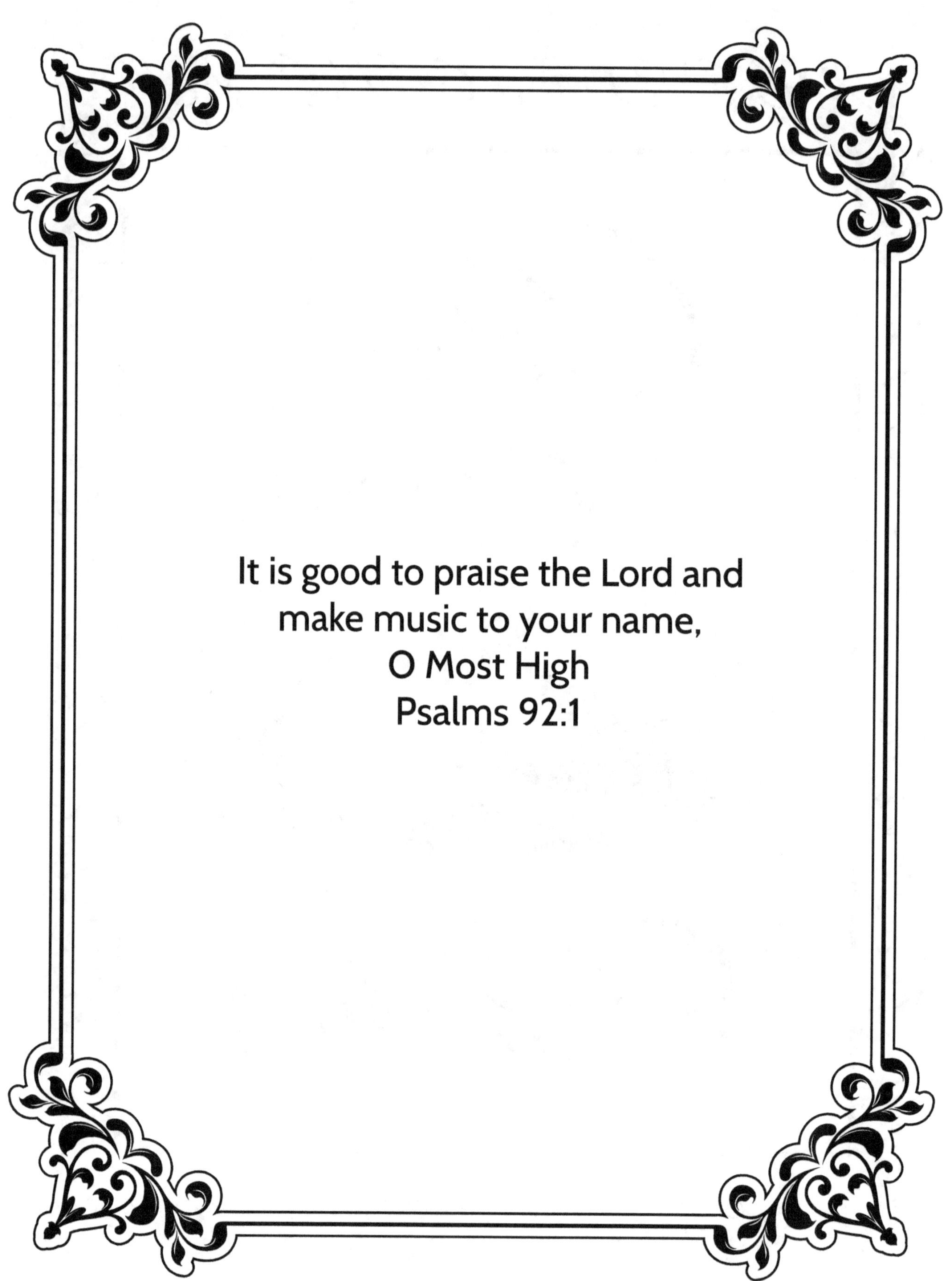

It is good to praise the Lord and
make music to your name,
O Most High
Psalms 92:1

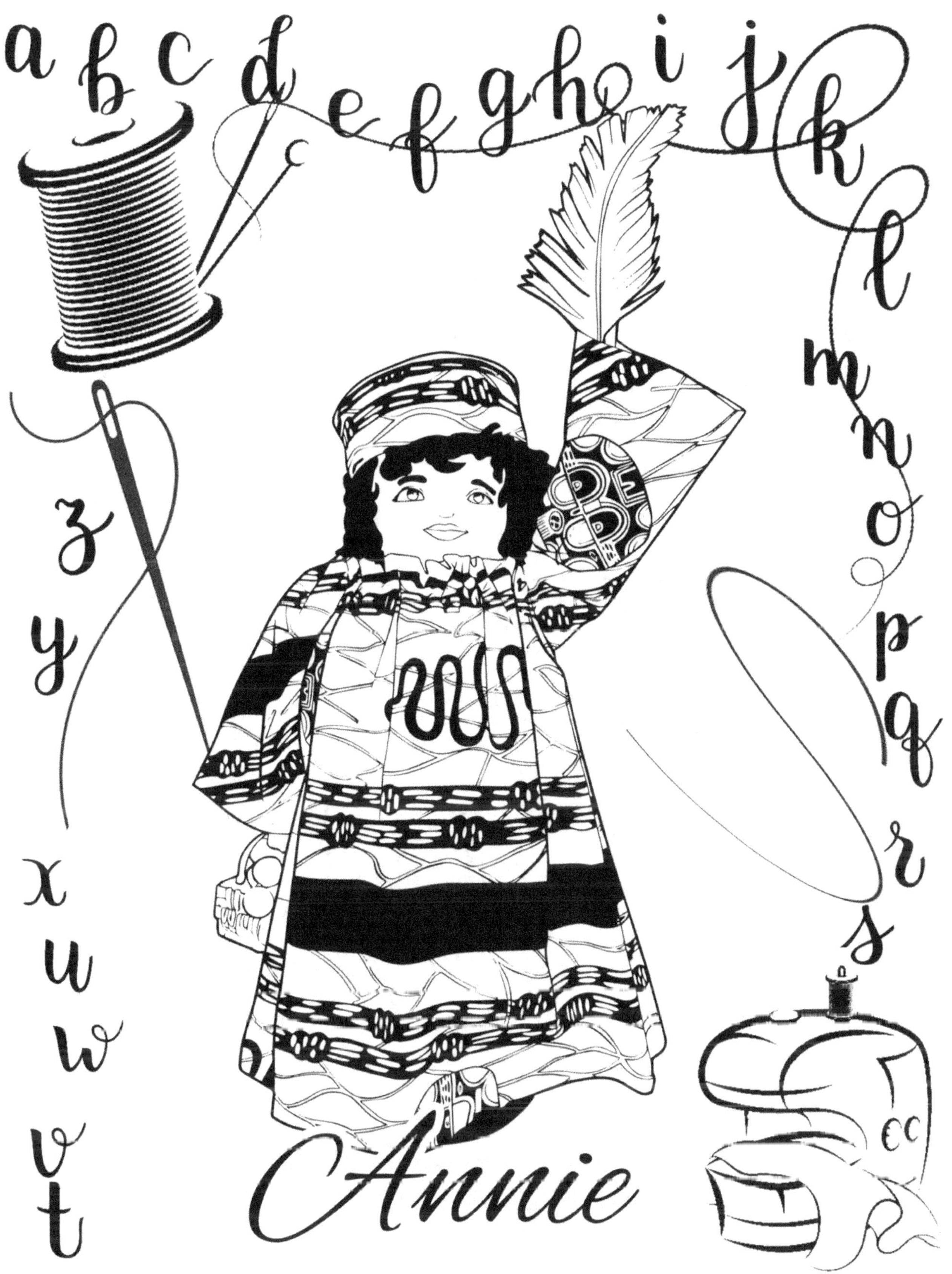
Annie

Luerine Madison Spencer

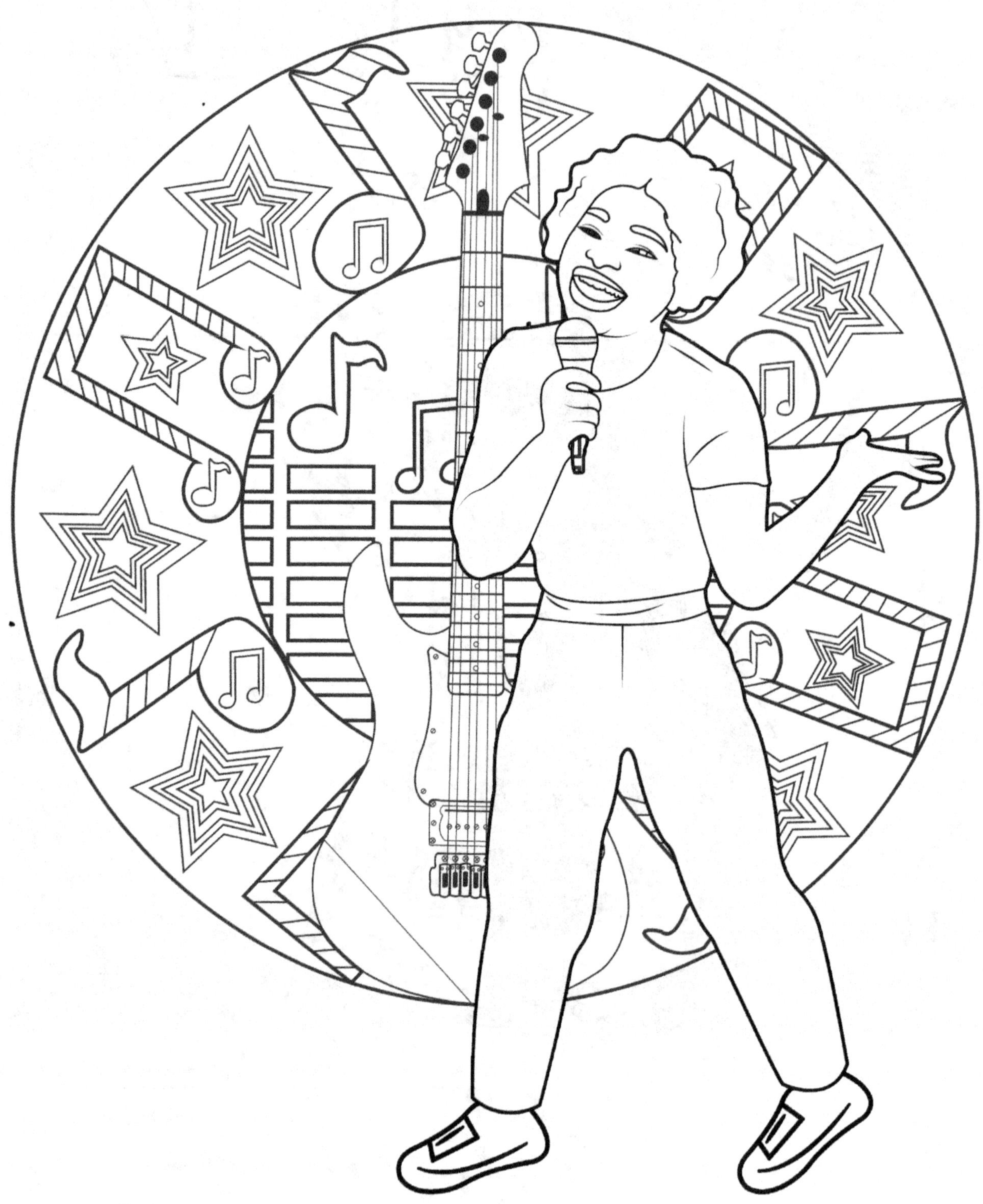

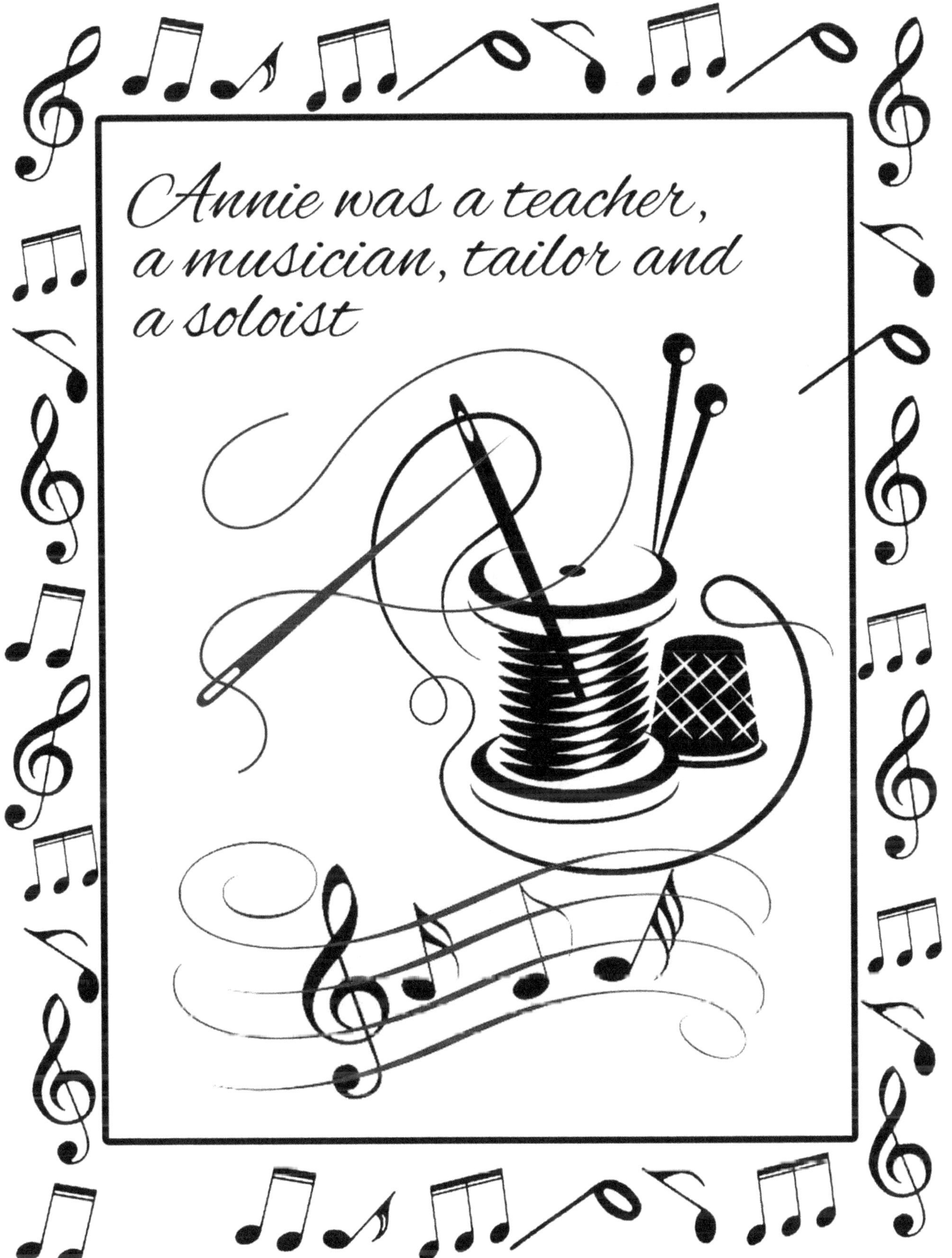

Annie was a teacher,
a musician, tailor and
a soloist

Luerine Madison Spencer

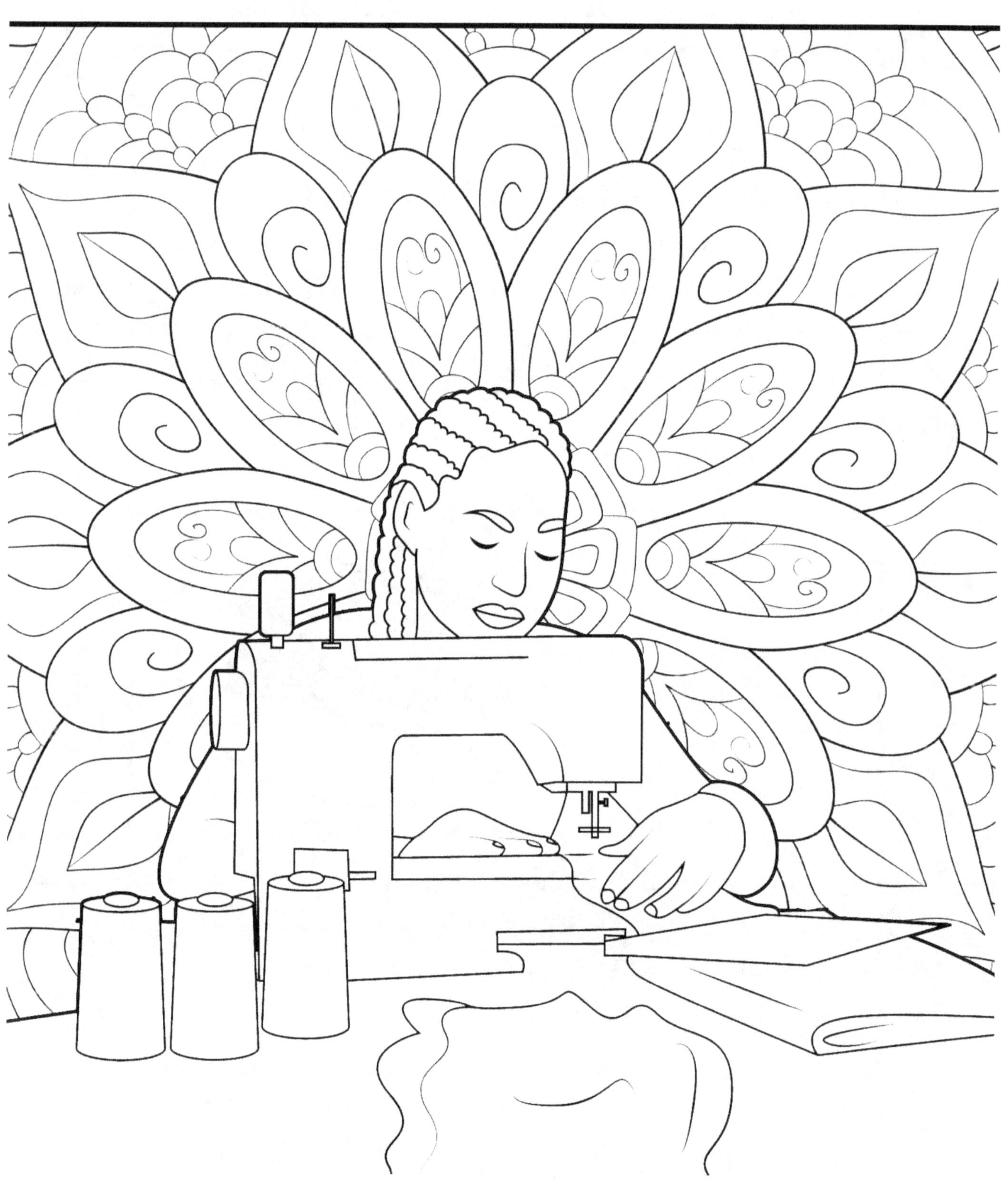

14

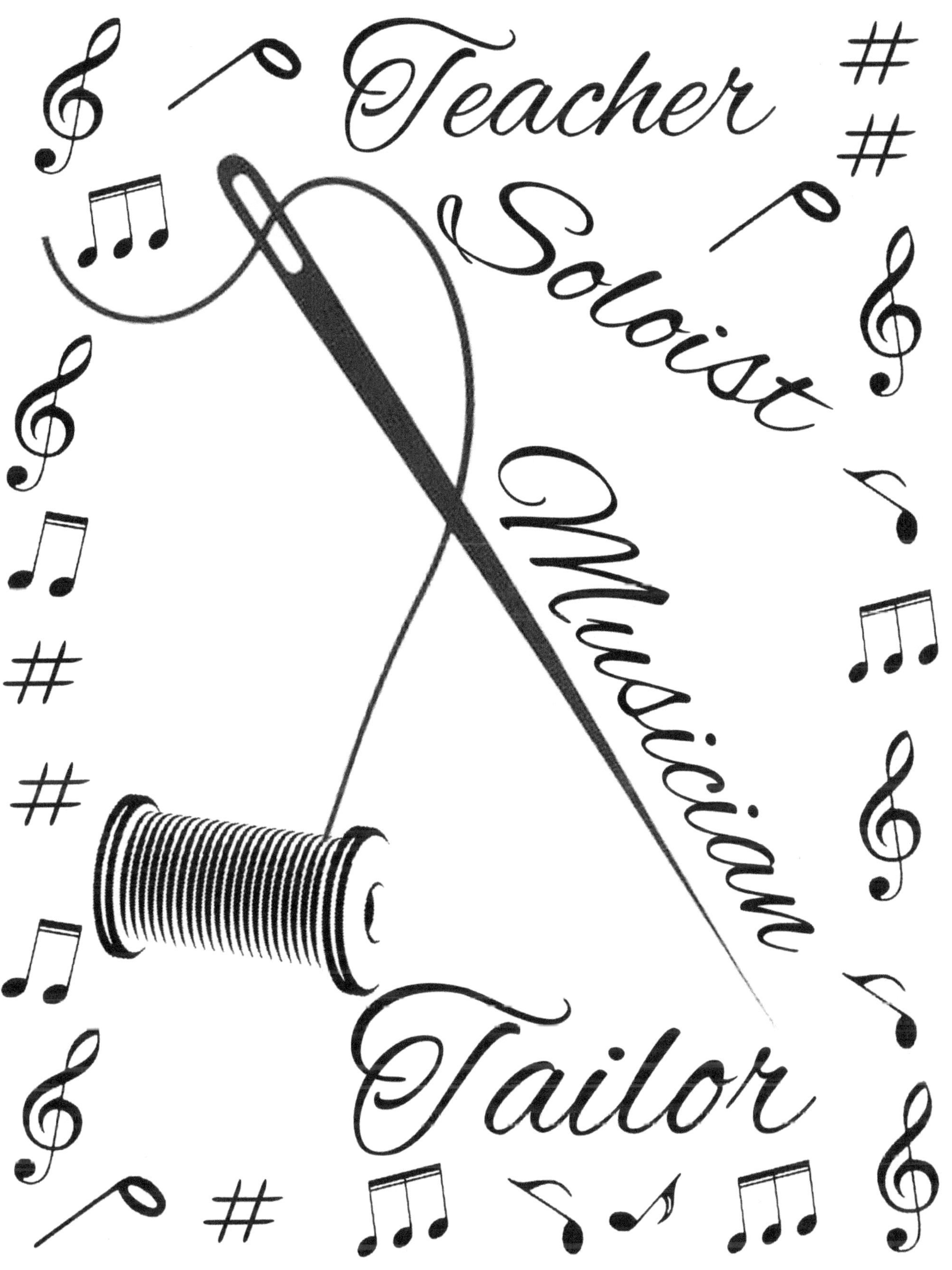
Teacher
Soloist
Musician
Tailor

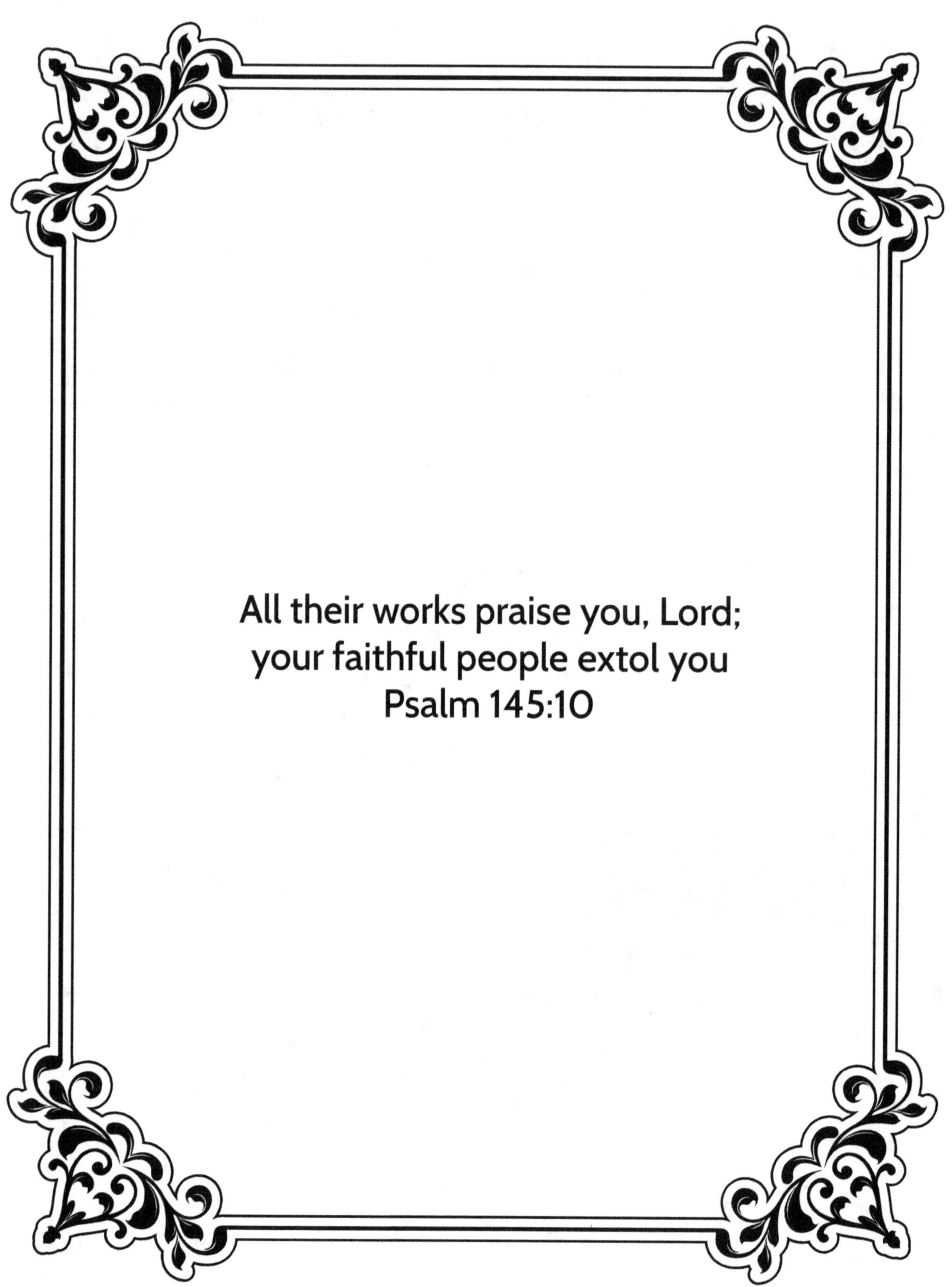

All their works praise you, Lord;
your faithful people extol you
Psalm 145:10

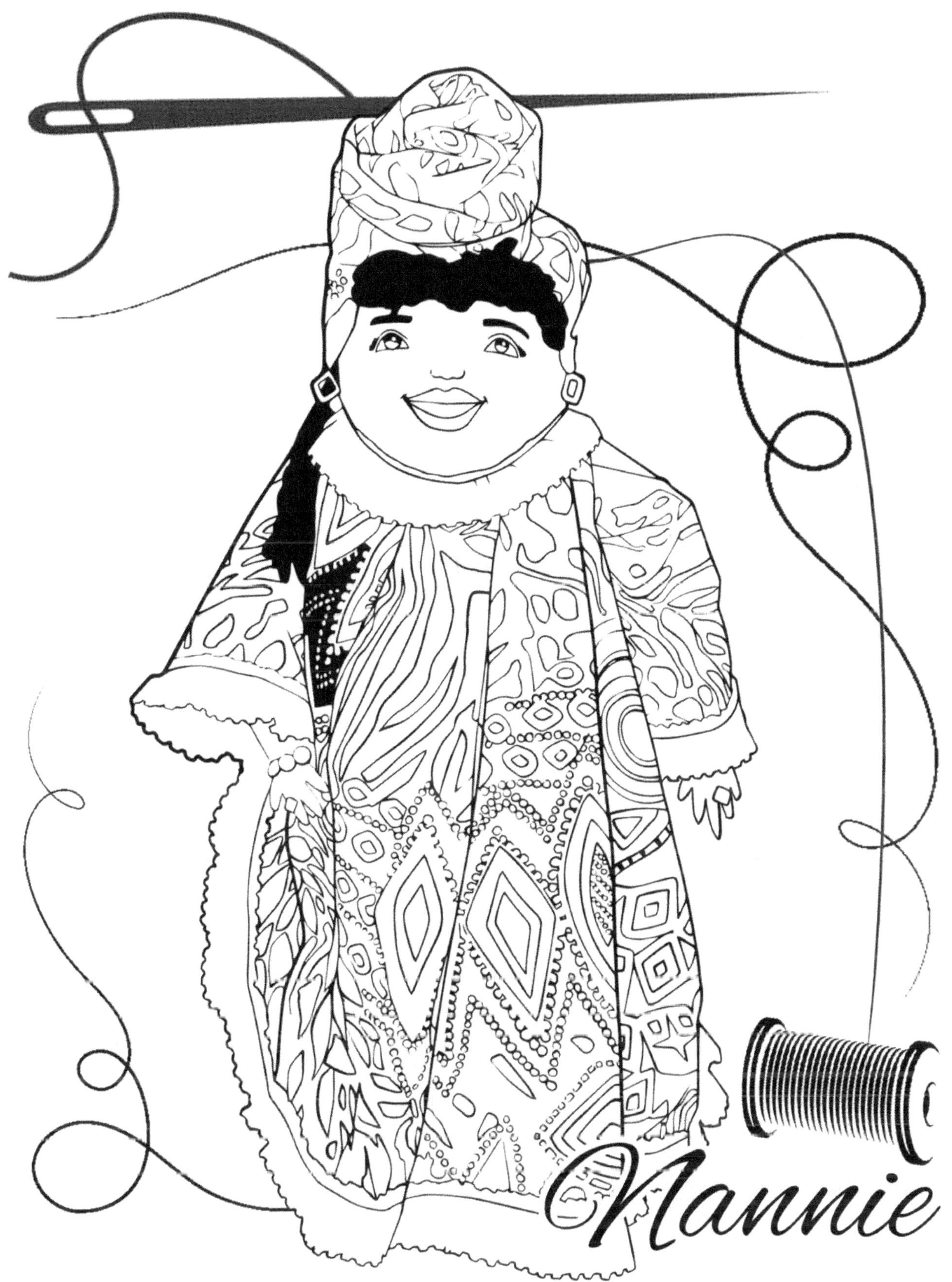

Nannie

Luerine Madison Spencer

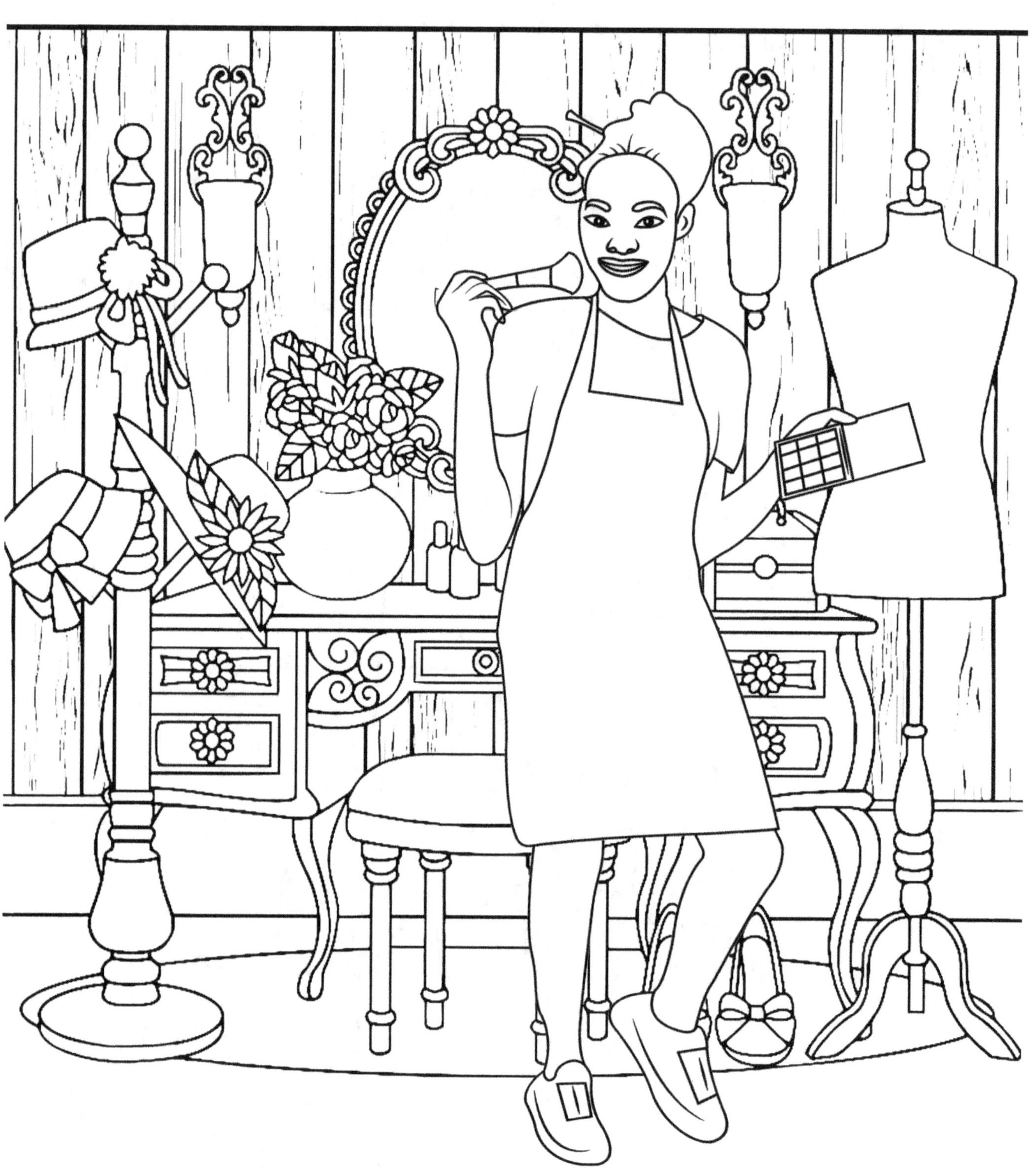

Nannie was a Secretary, Soloist, Tailor, Beautician and a Musician

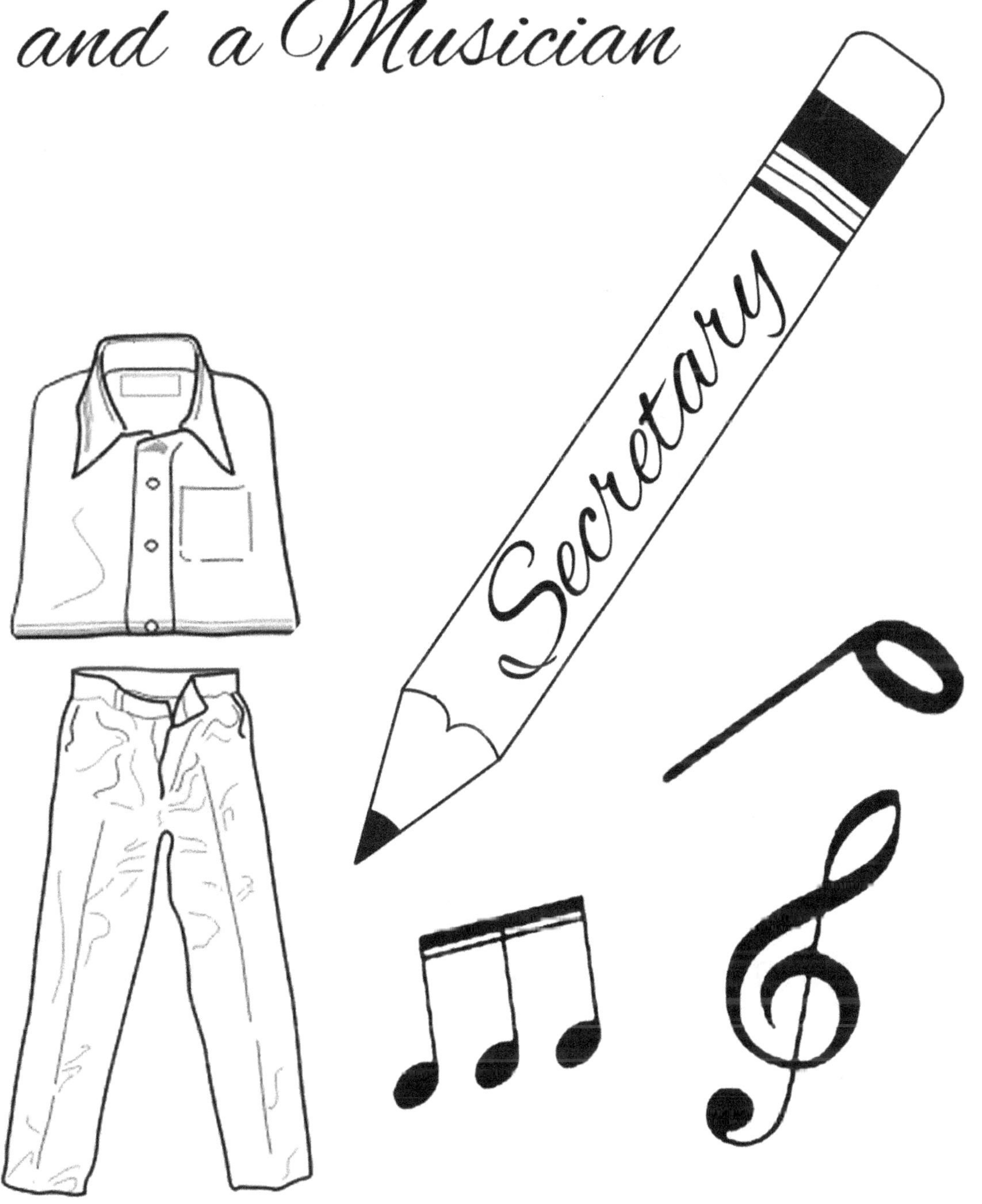

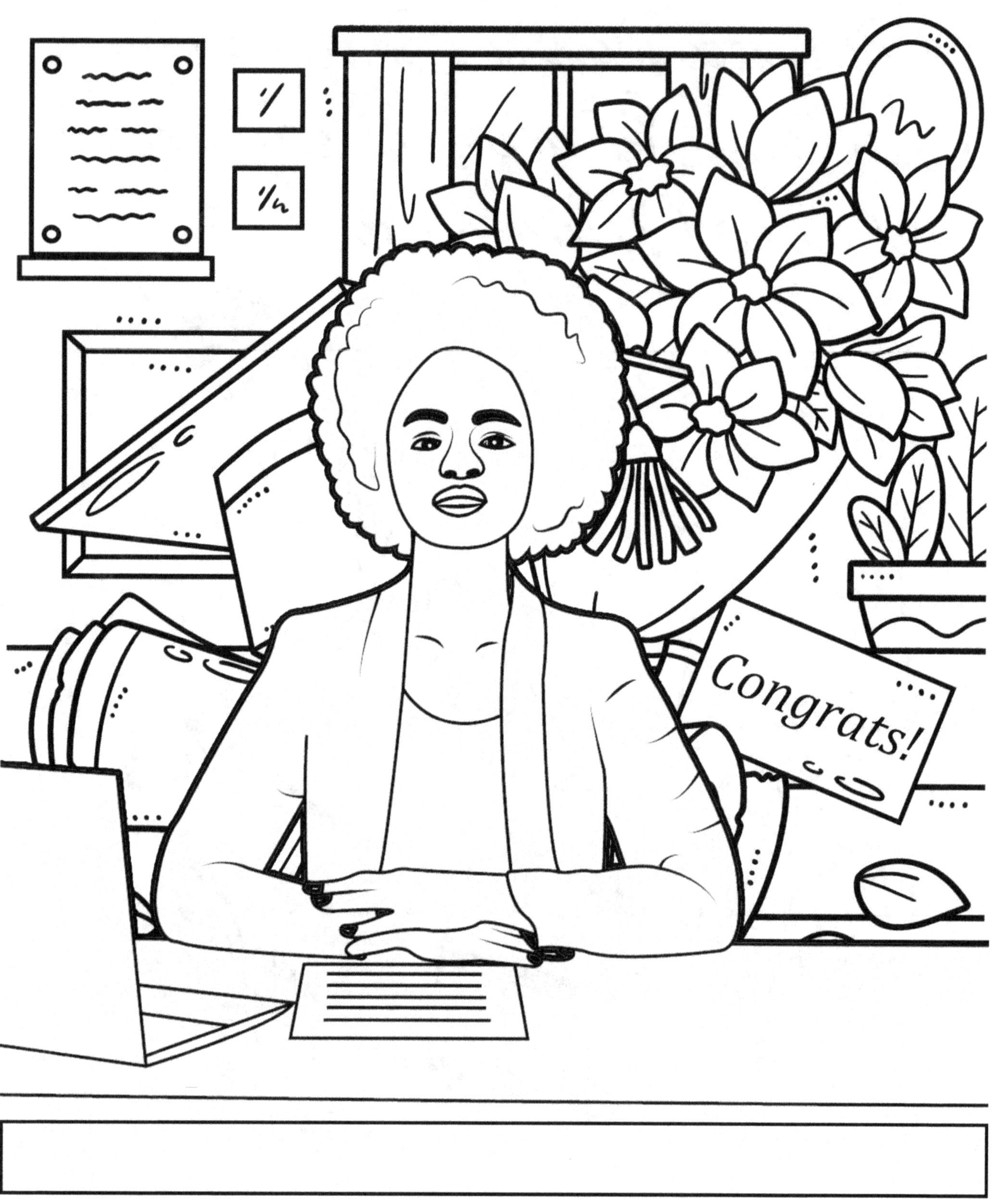

Congrats!

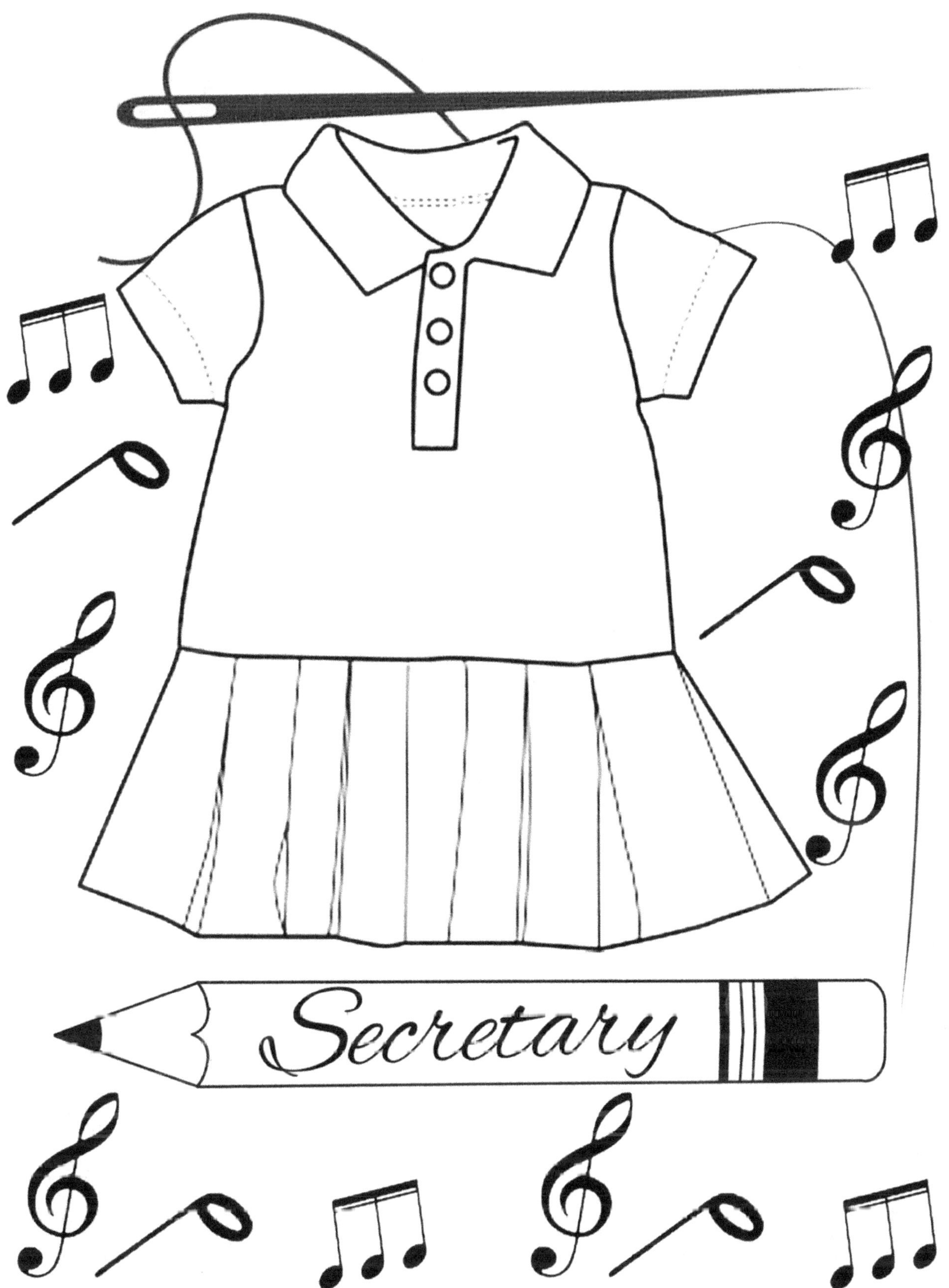
Secretary

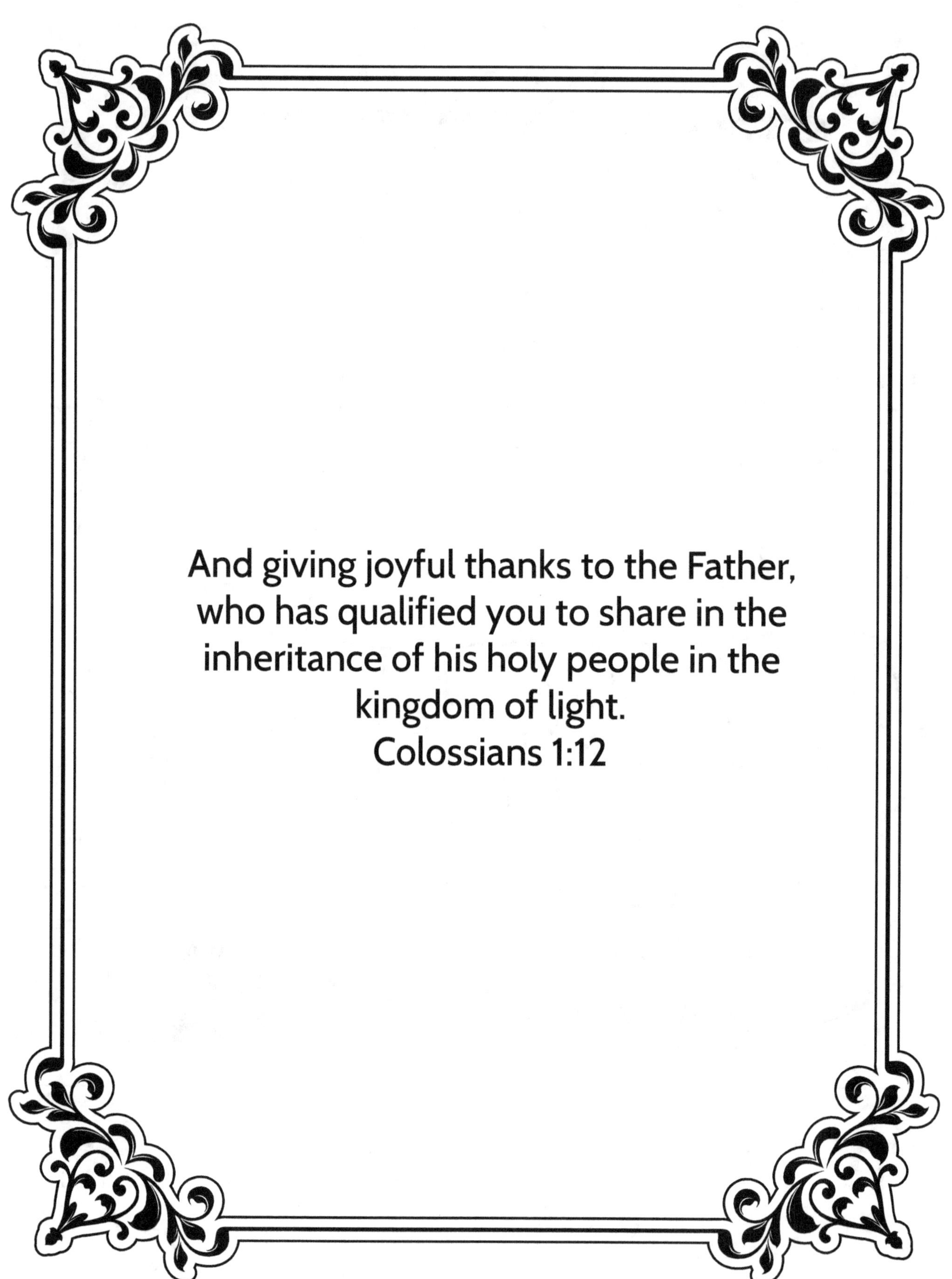

And giving joyful thanks to the Father,
who has qualified you to share in the
inheritance of his holy people in the
kingdom of light.
Colossians 1:12

Luerine Madison Spencer

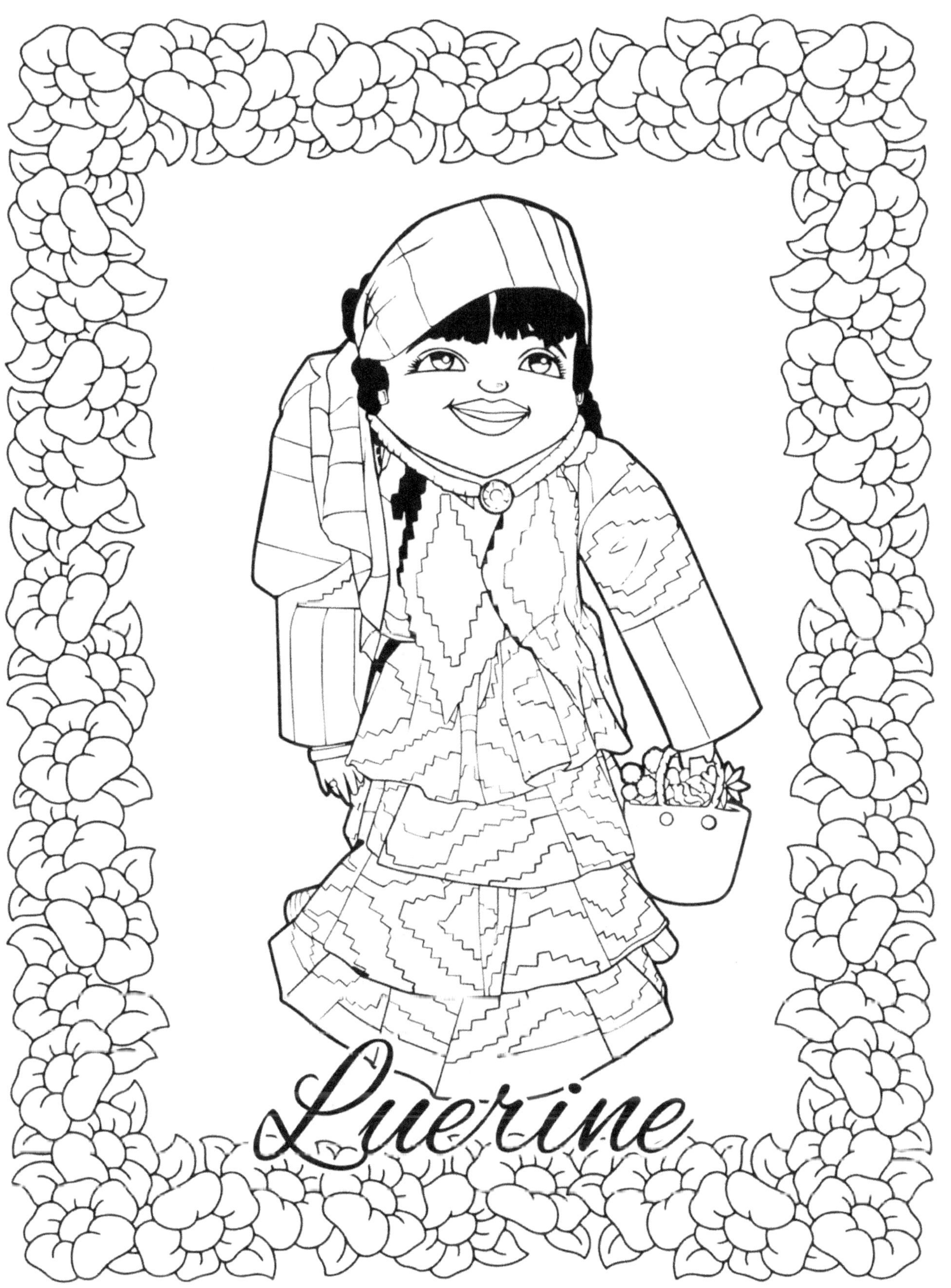
Luerine

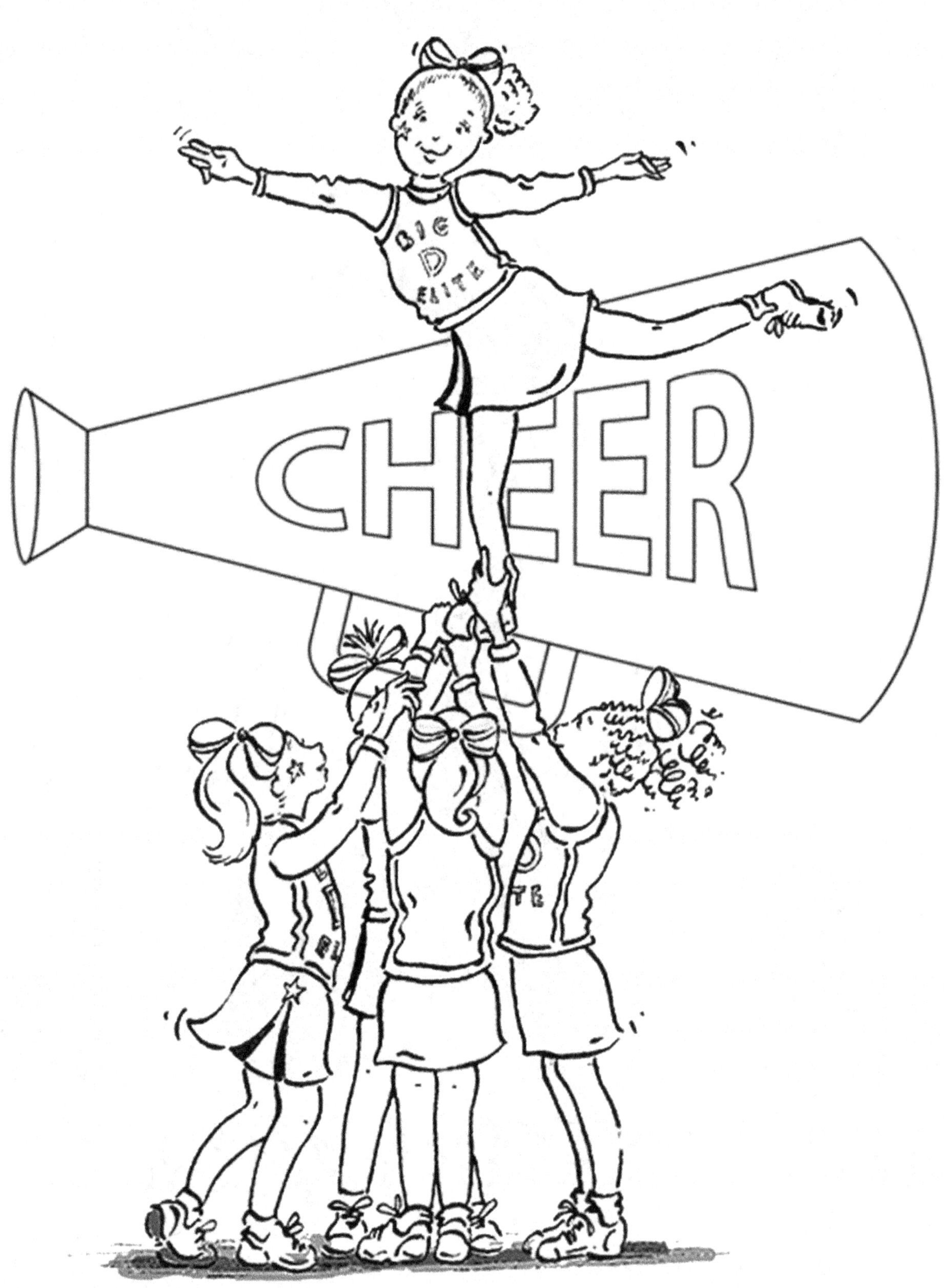

BIG
D
ELITE
CHEER

Luerine was a Cheerleader, Soloist drummer, Art Teacher, a decorator and Tailor

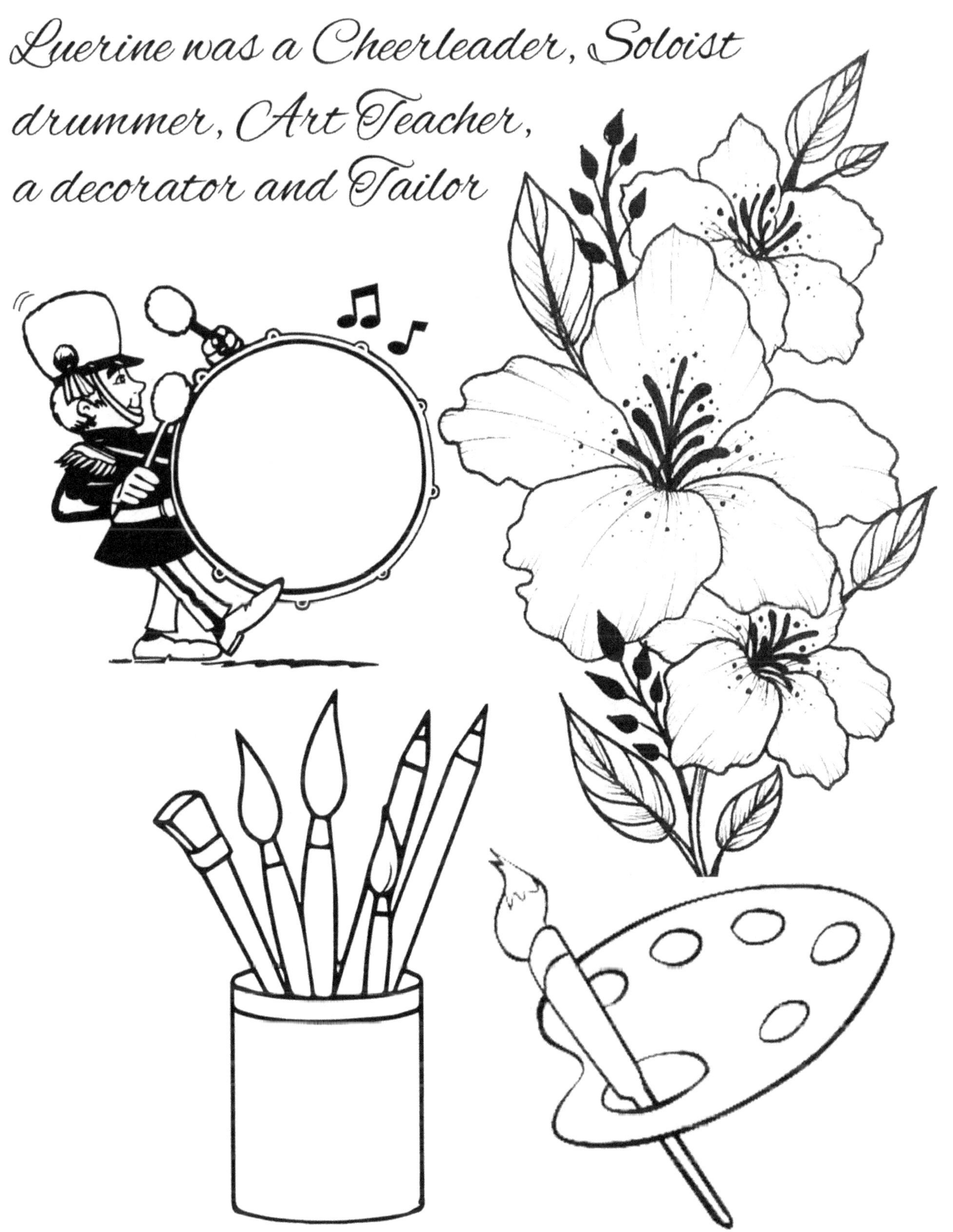

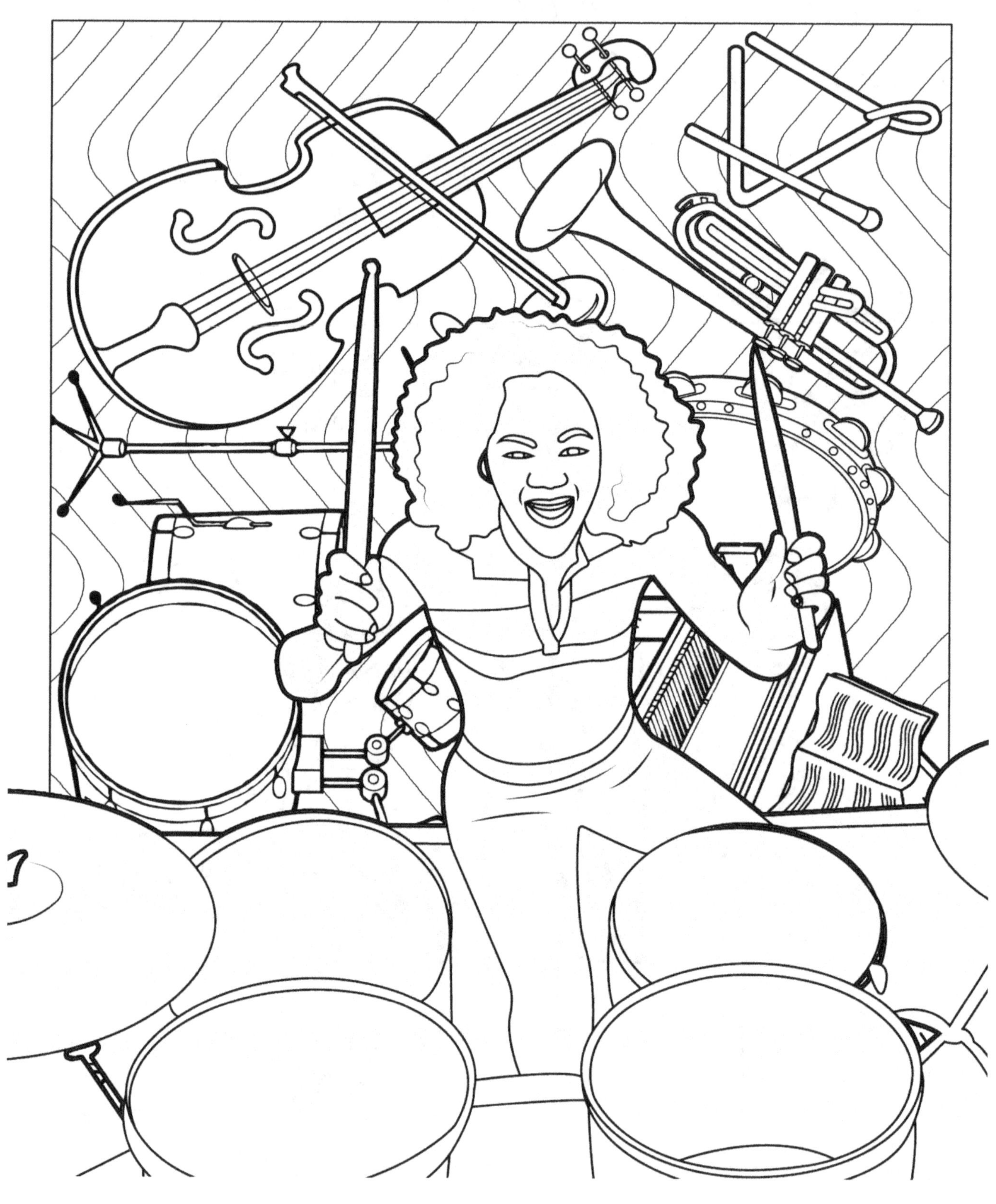

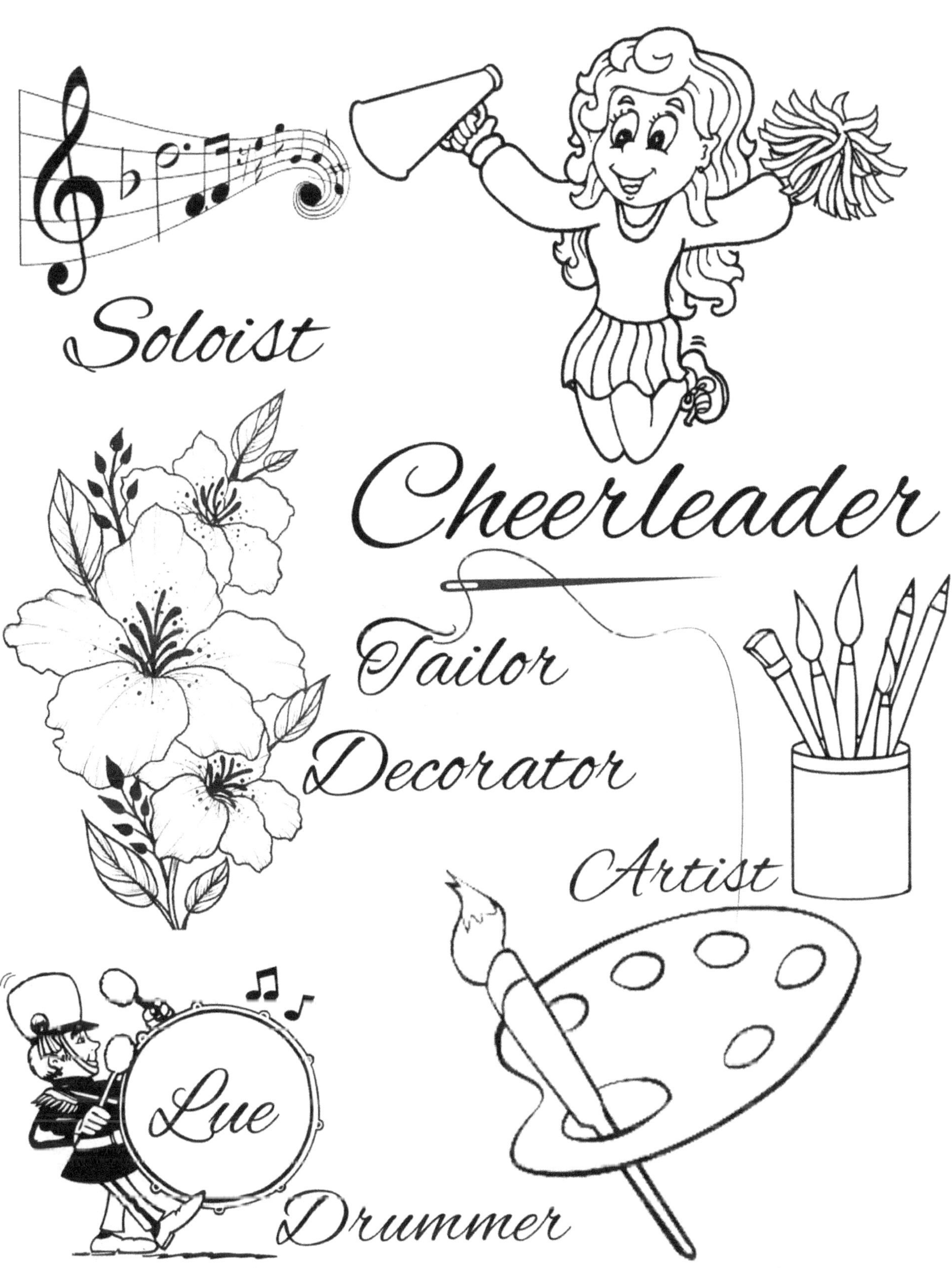

Soloist
Cheerleader
Tailor
Decorator
Artist
Lue
Drummer

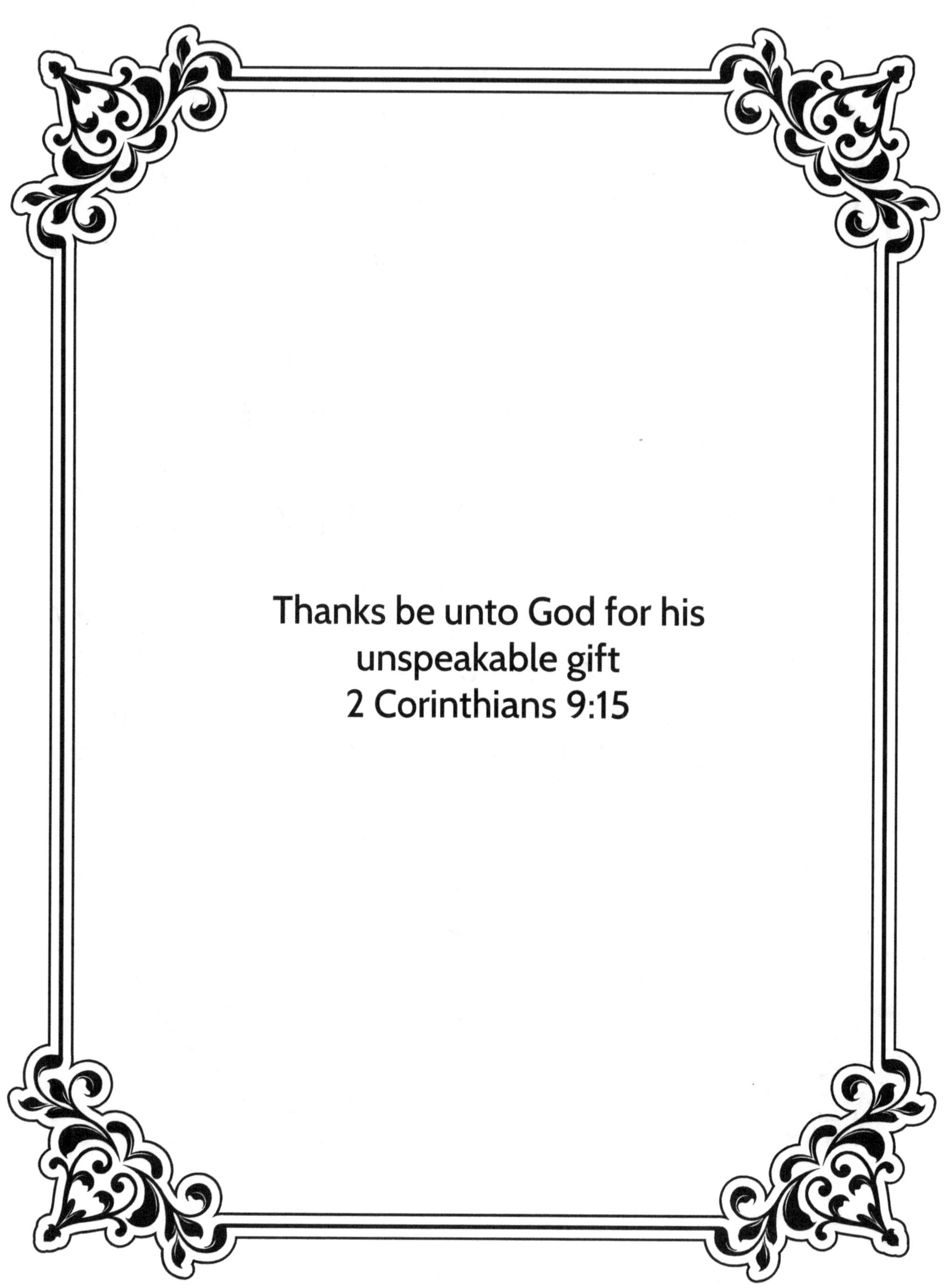

Luerine Madison Spencer

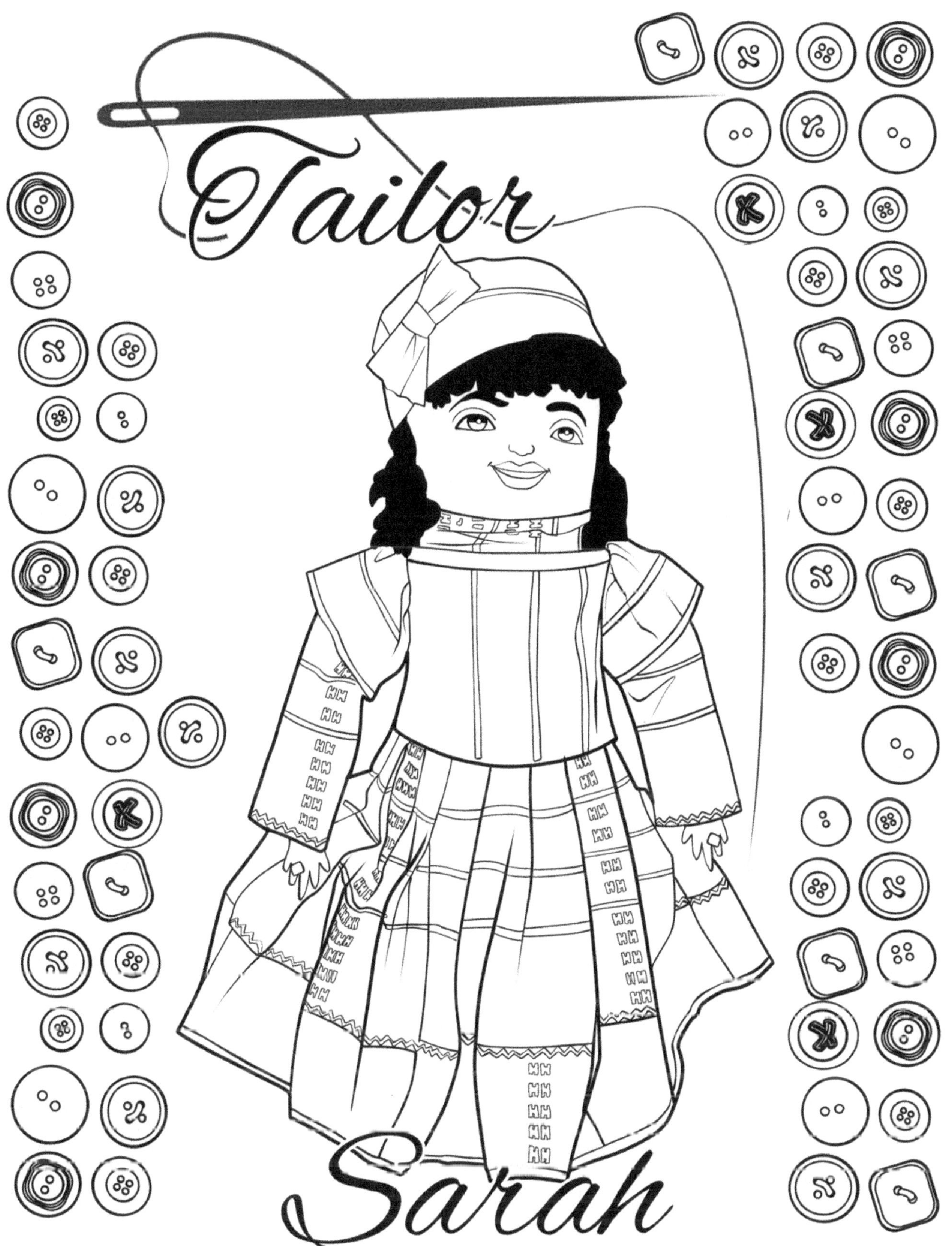
Tailor
Sarah

Luerine Madison Spencer

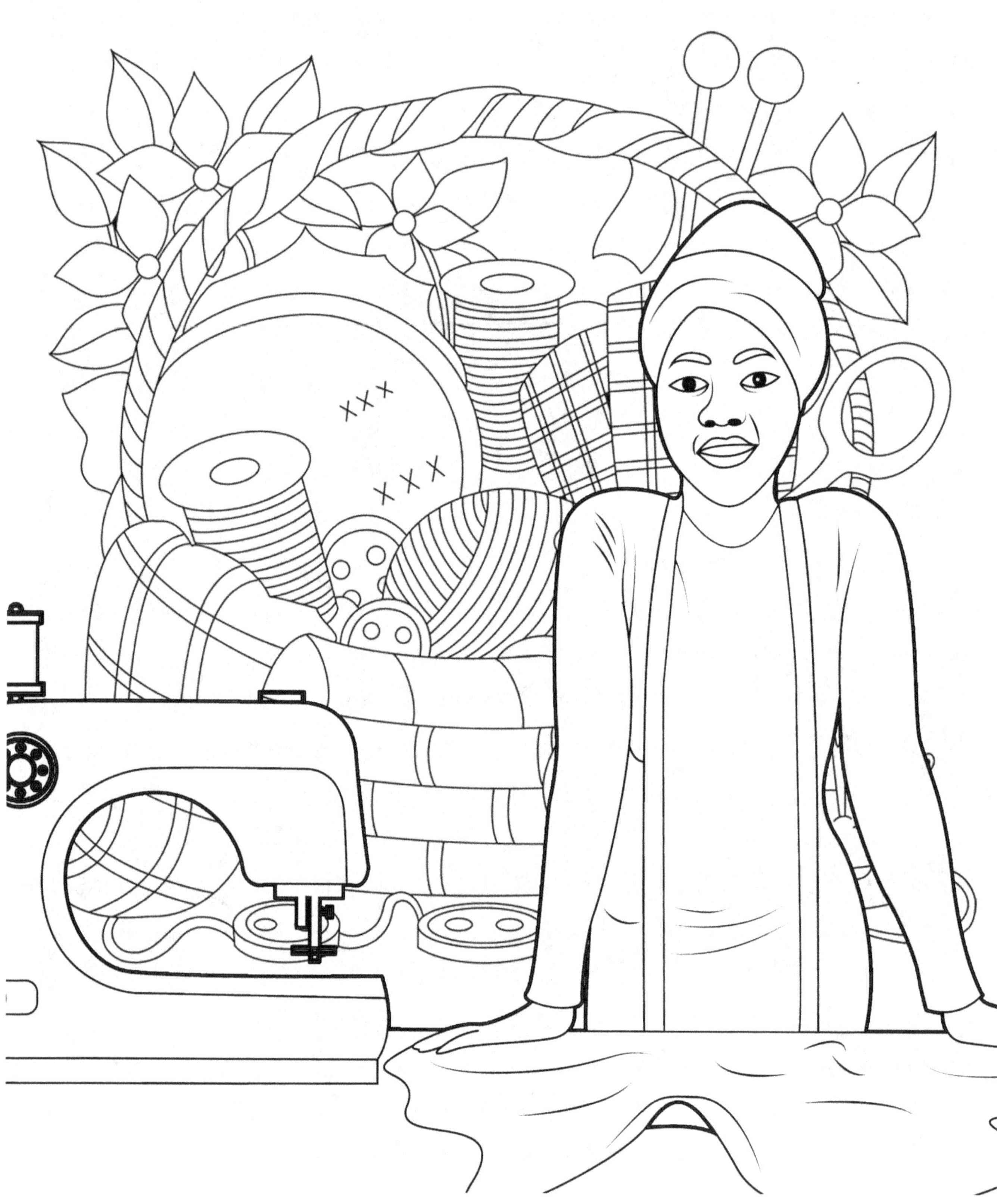

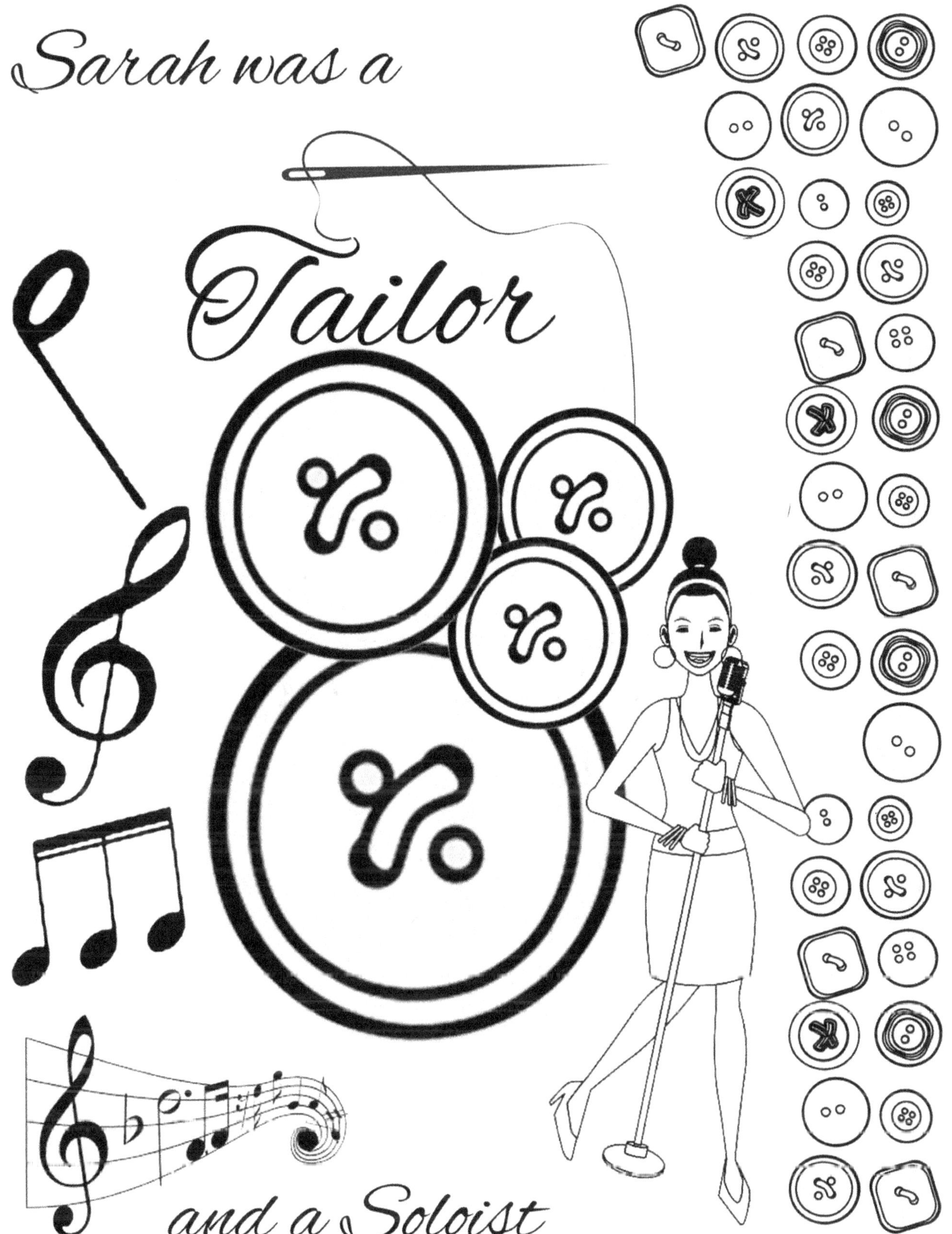
Sarah was a
Tailor
and a Soloist

Luerine Madison Spencer

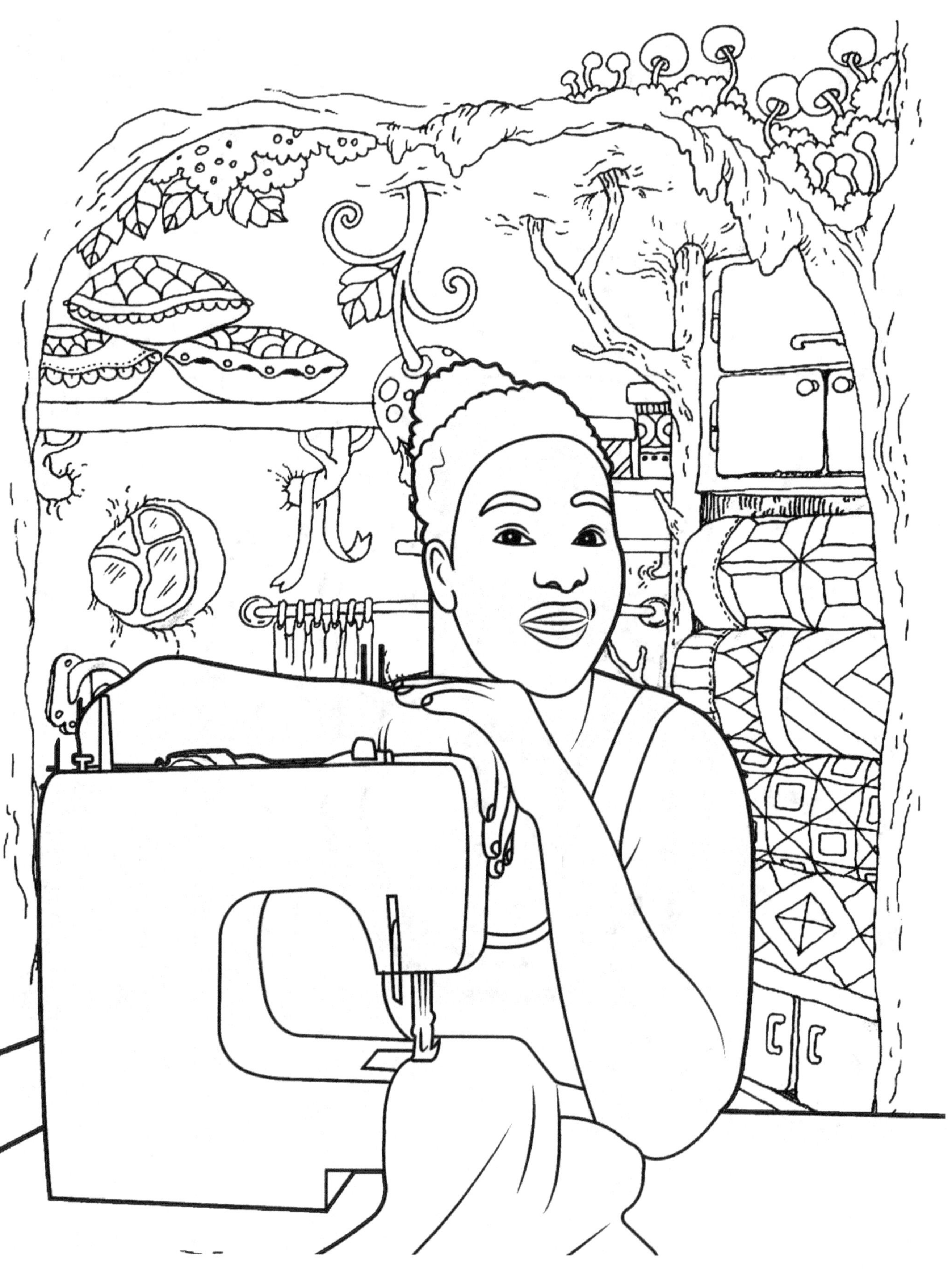

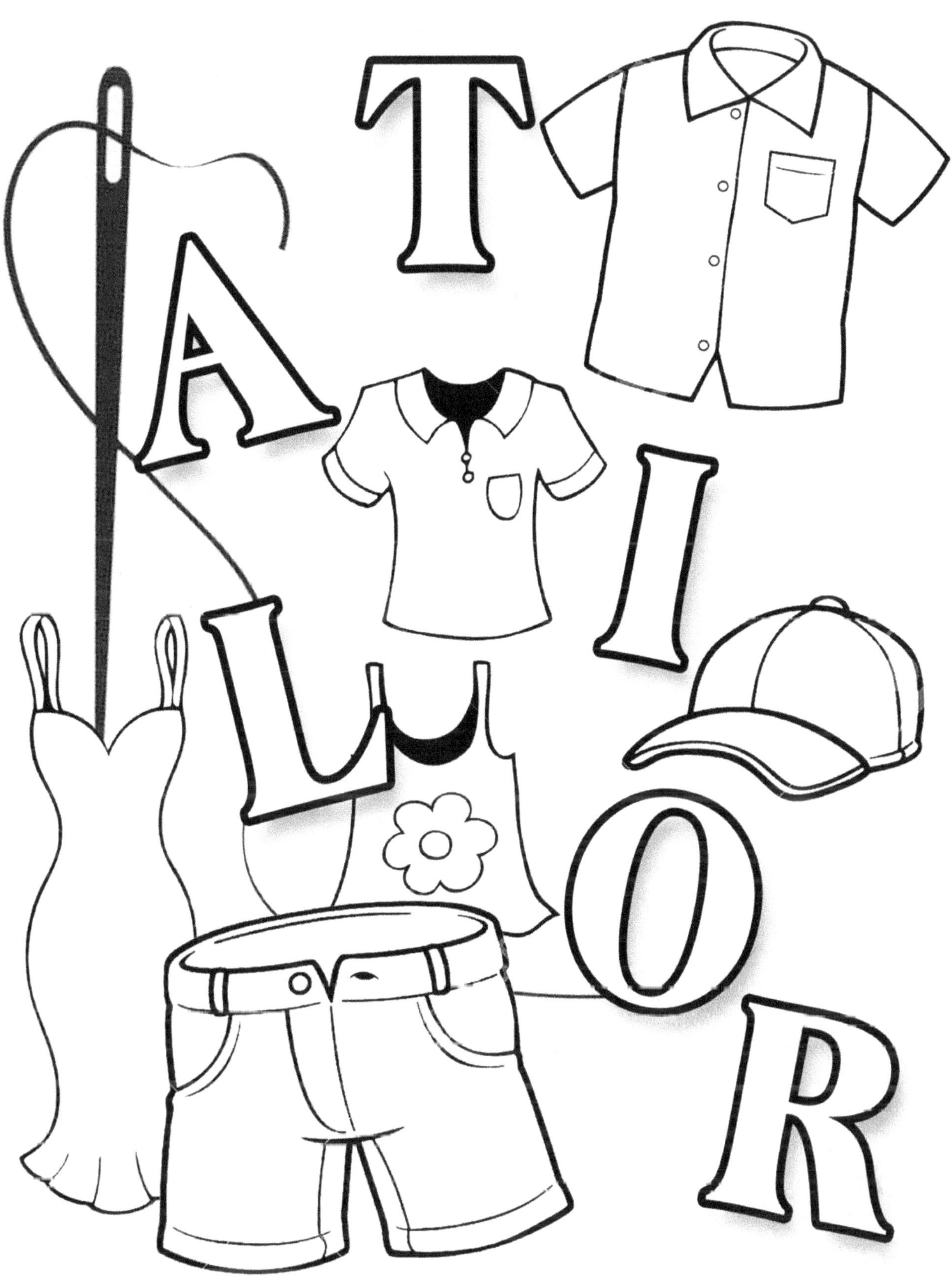

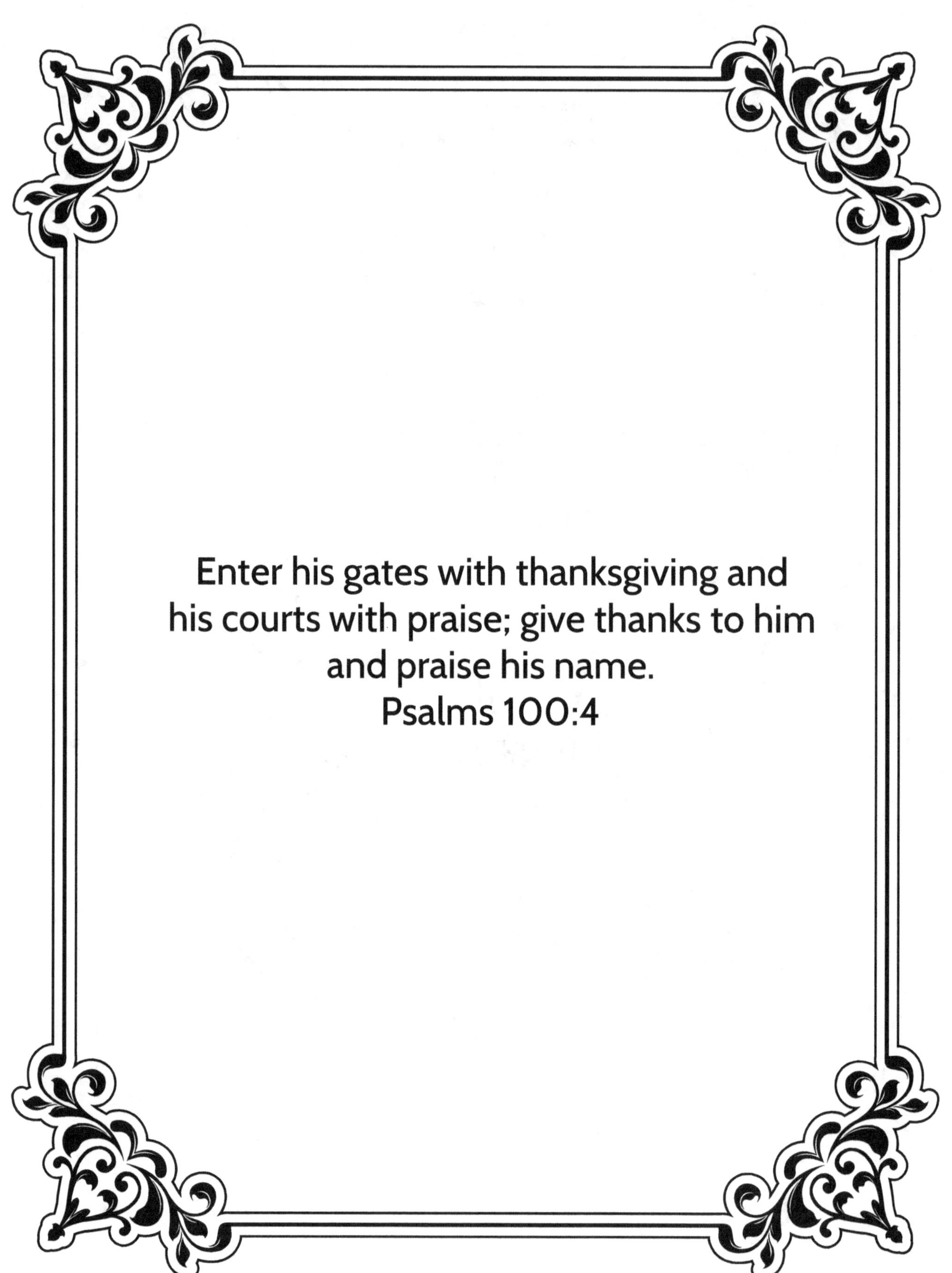
Enter his gates with thanksgiving and
his courts with praise; give thanks to him
and praise his name.
Psalms 100:4
Luerine Madison Spencer

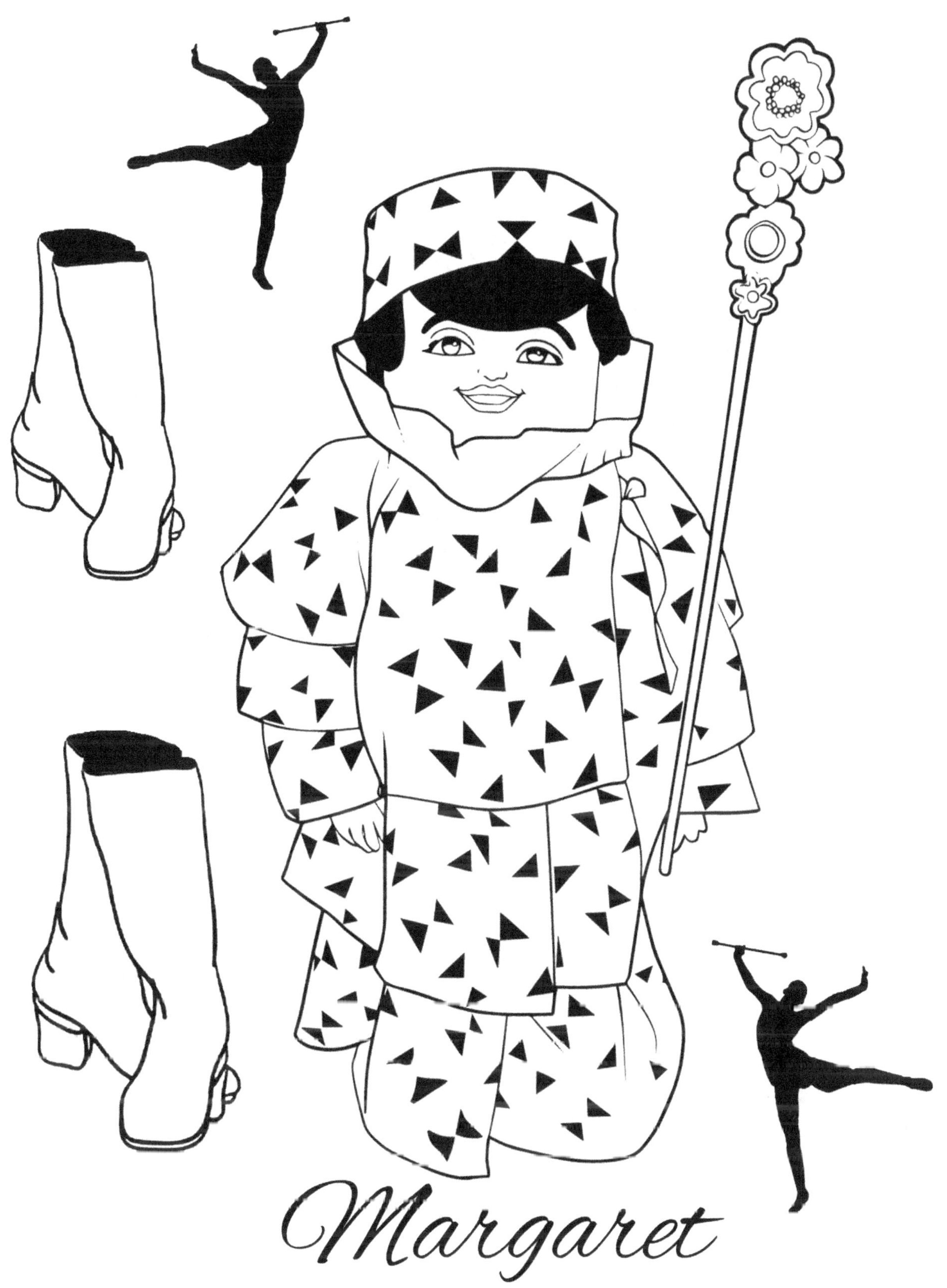

Margaret

Luerine Madison Spencer

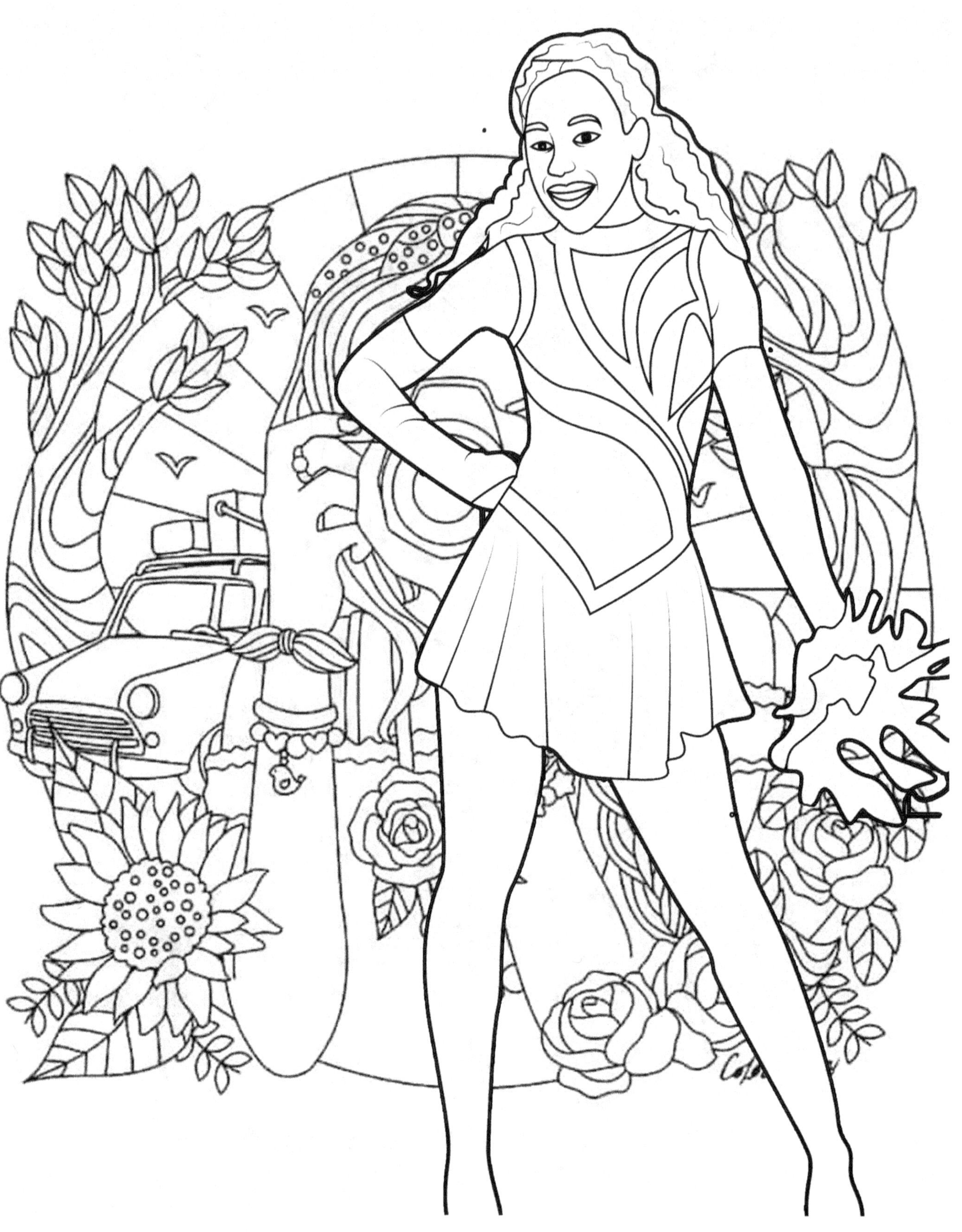

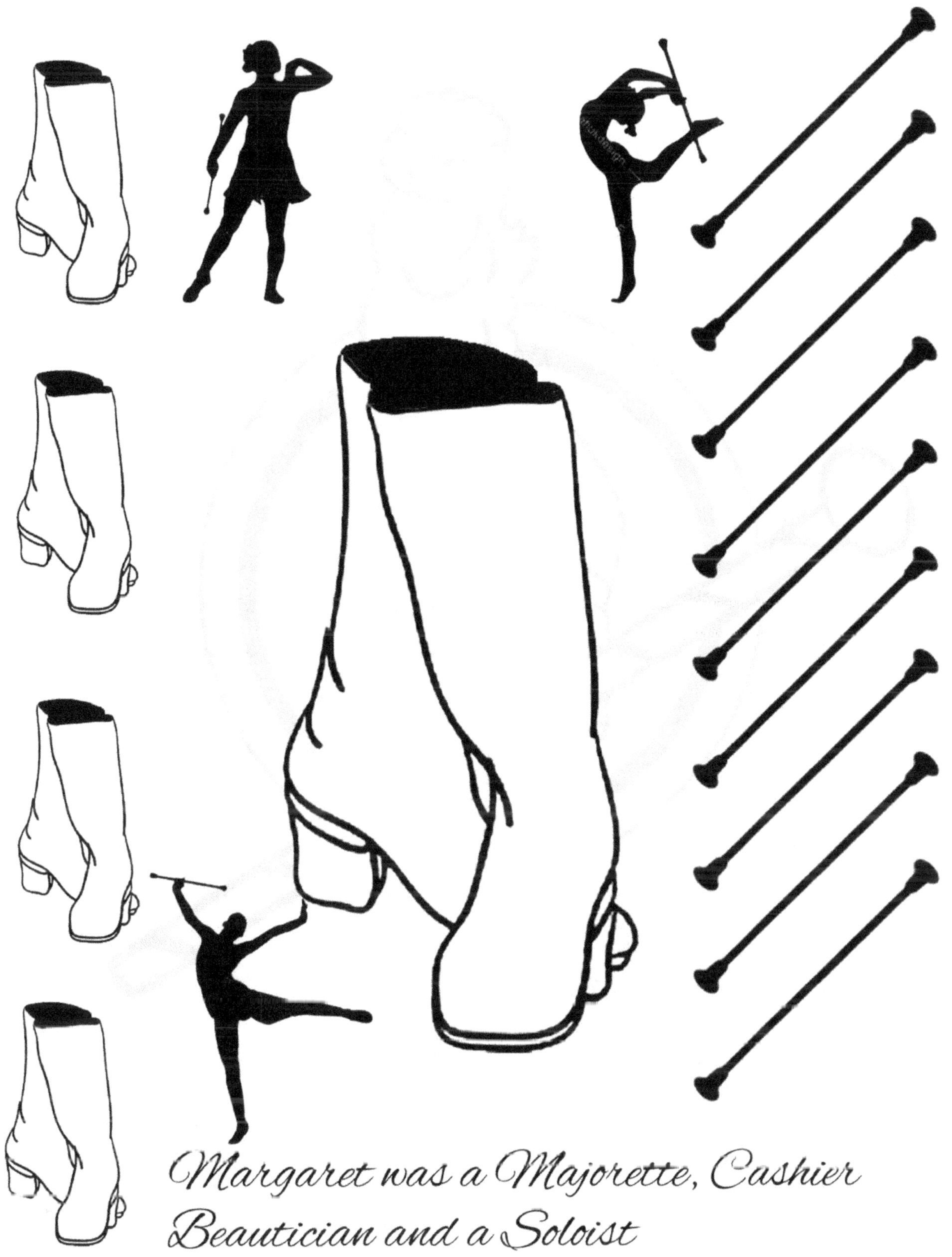

Margaret was a Majorette, Cashier Beautician and a Soloist

Luerine Madison Spencer

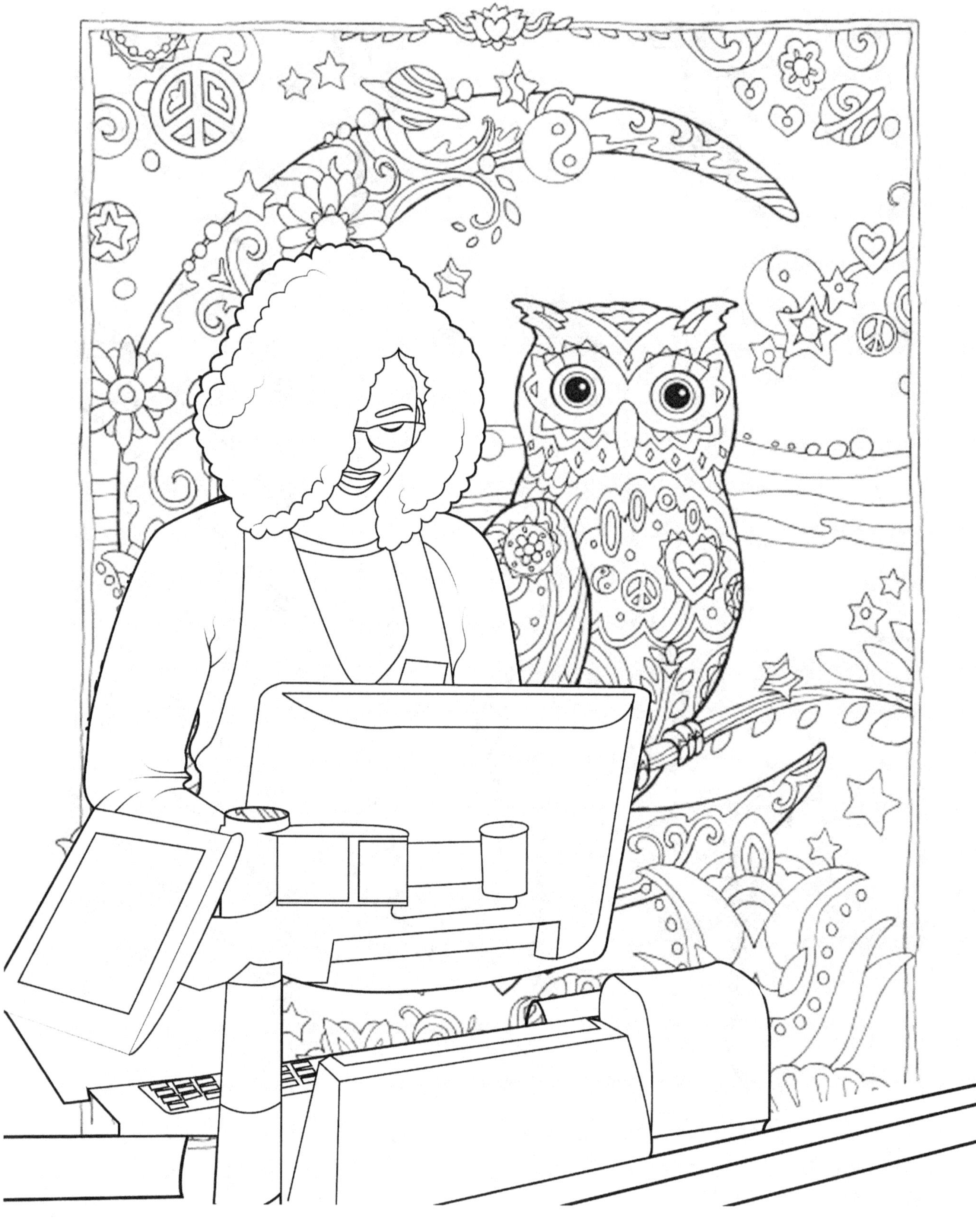

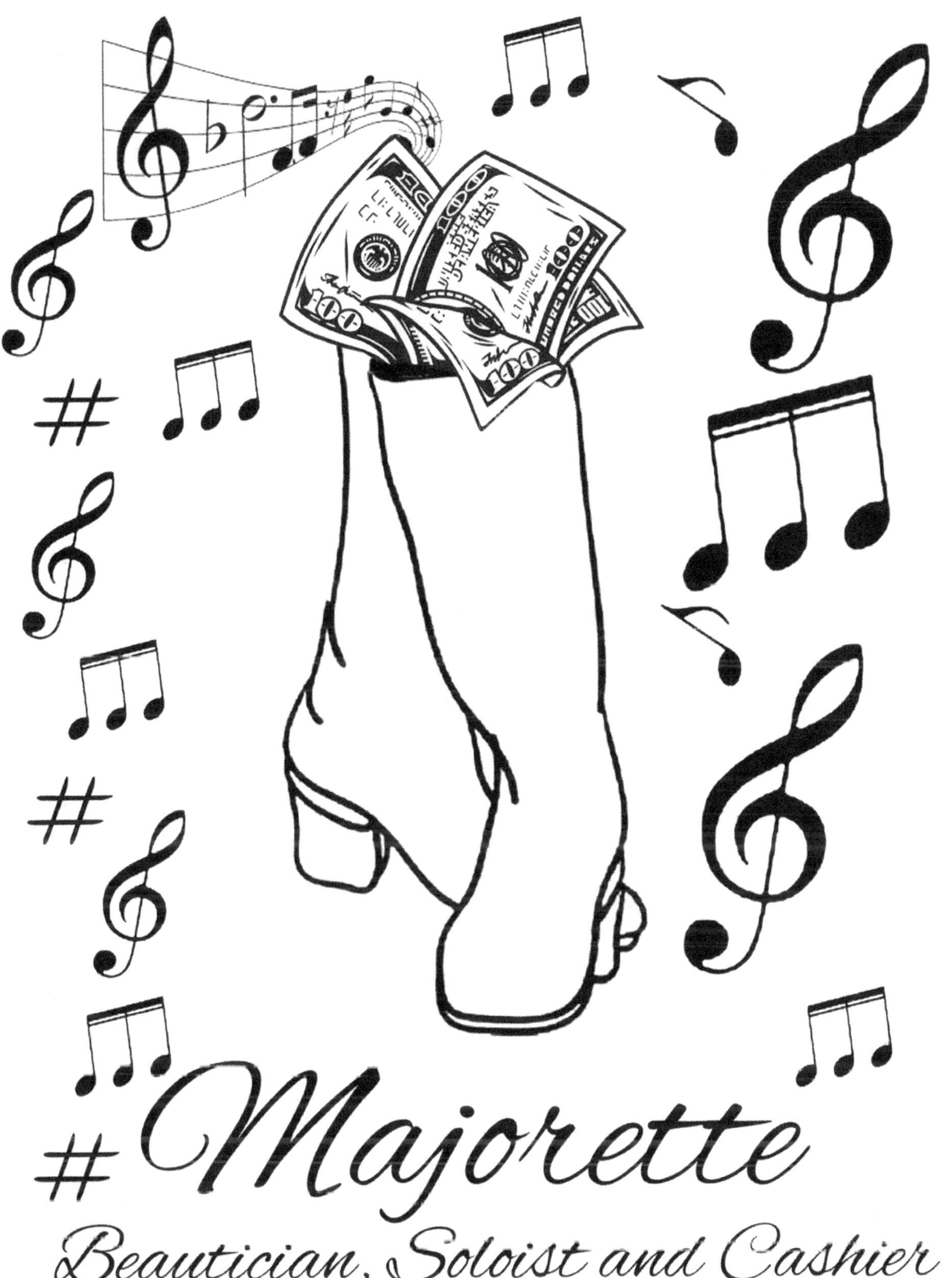

#Majorette

Beautician, Soloist and Cashier

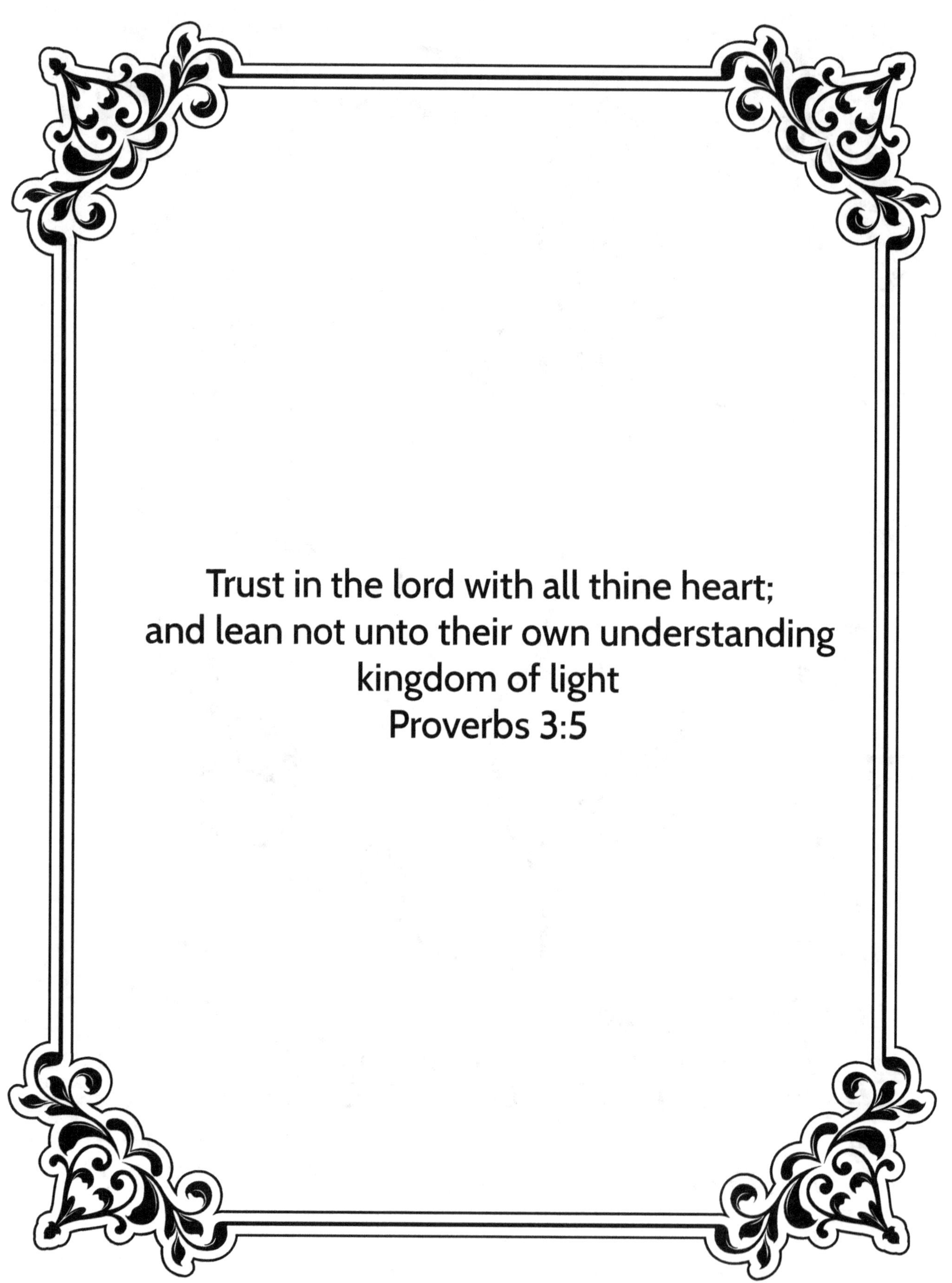
Trust in the lord with all thine heart;
and lean not unto their own understanding
kingdom of light
Proverbs 3:5

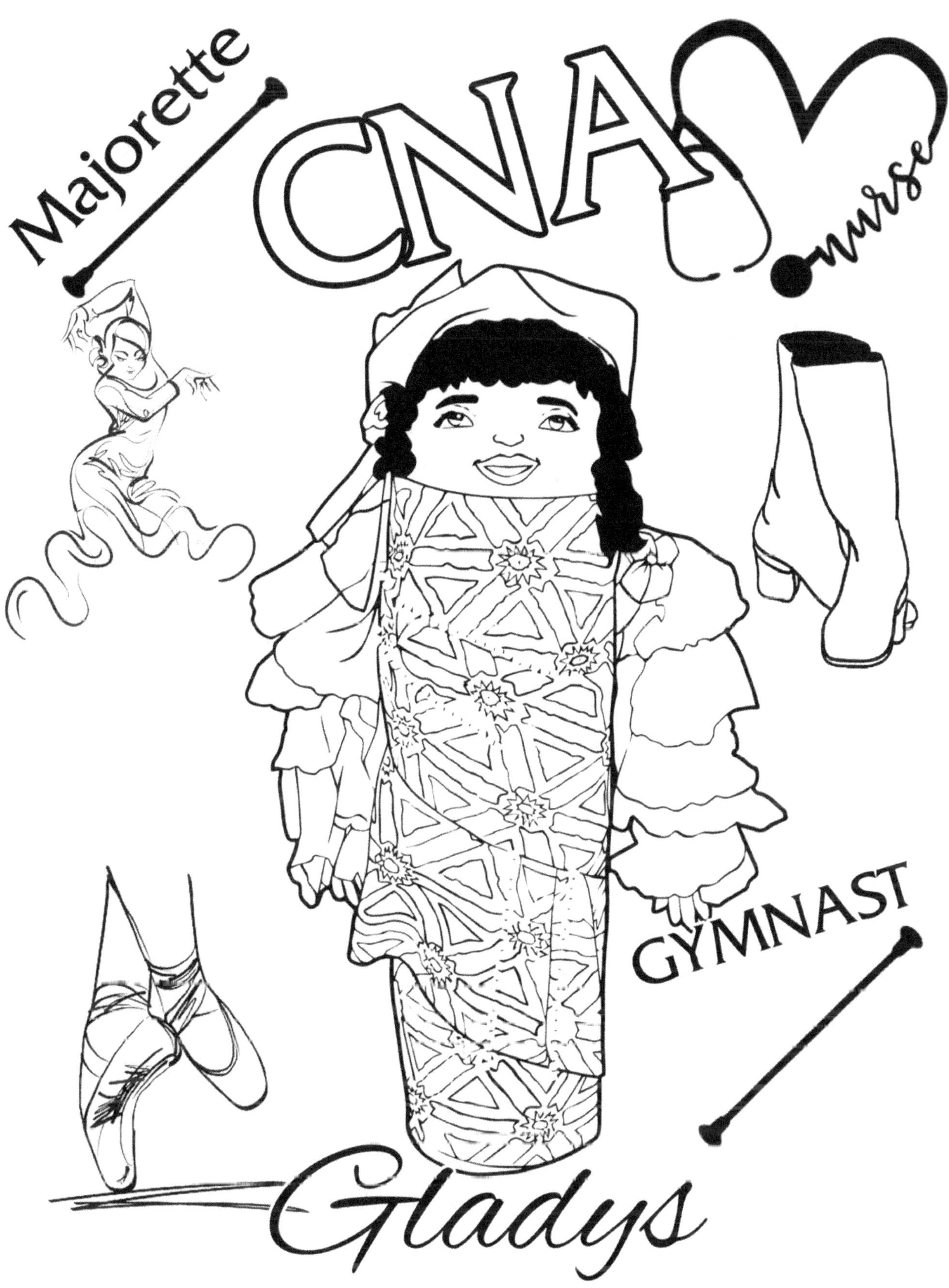

Majorette
CNA
nurse
GYMNAST
Gladys

Luerine Madison Spencer

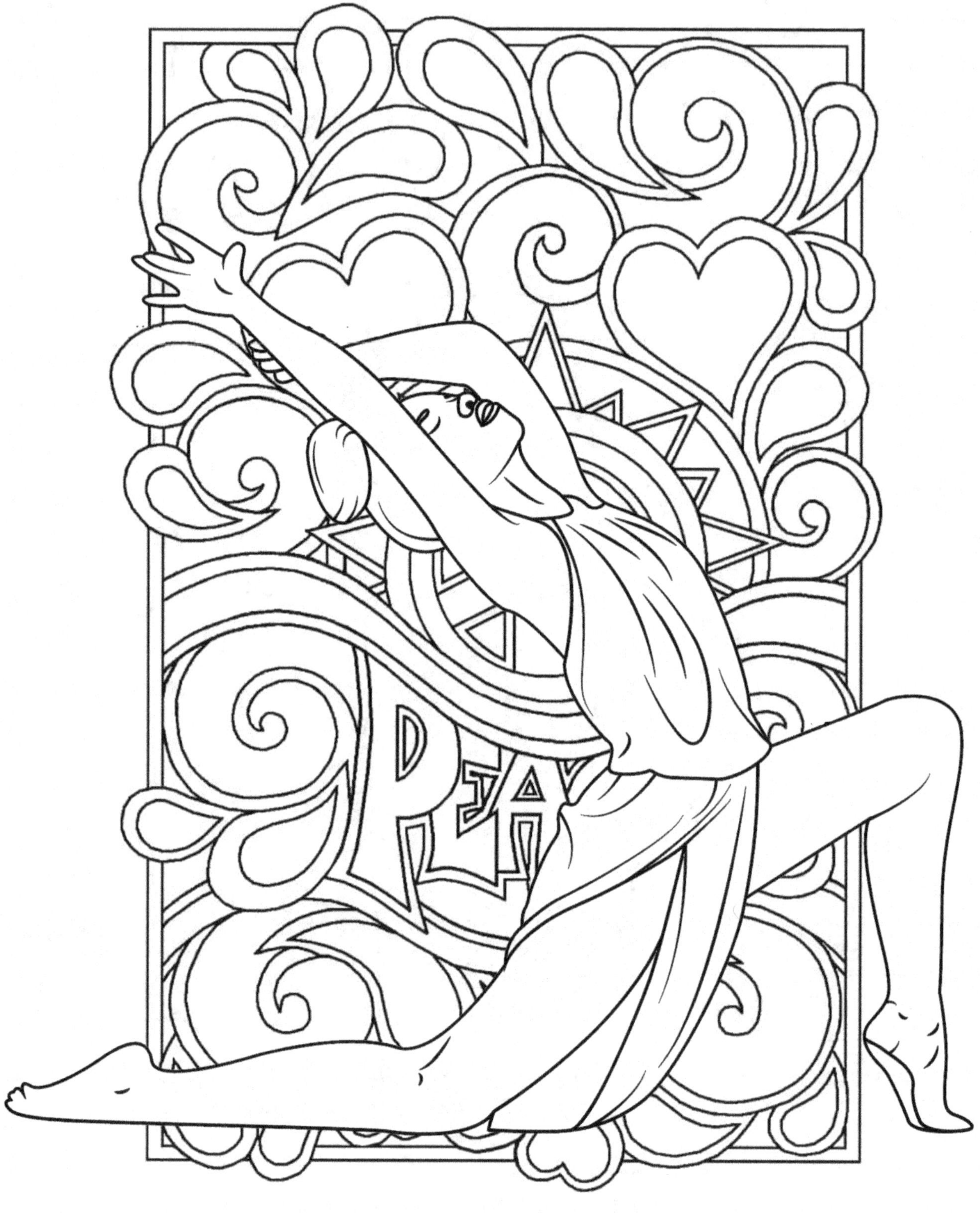

Gladys was a Dancer, Gymnast Majorette, Tailor and a CNA

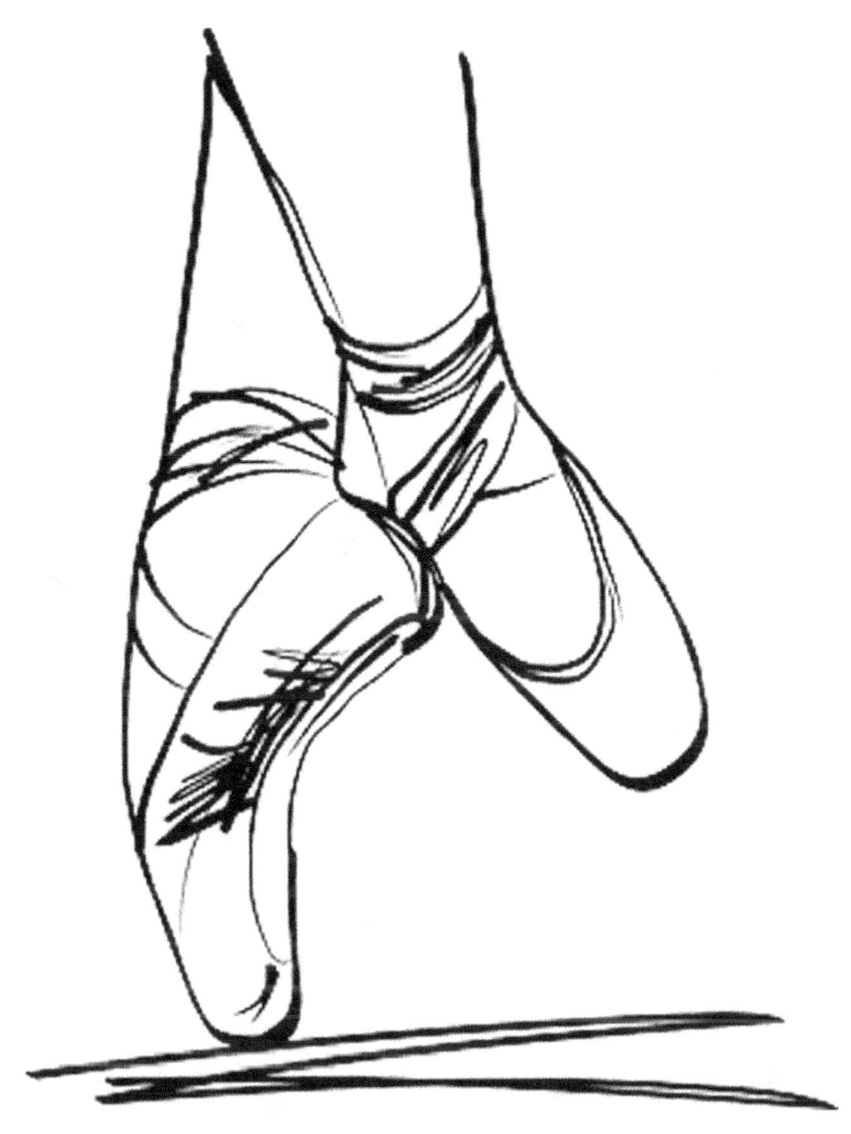

Luerine Madison Spencer

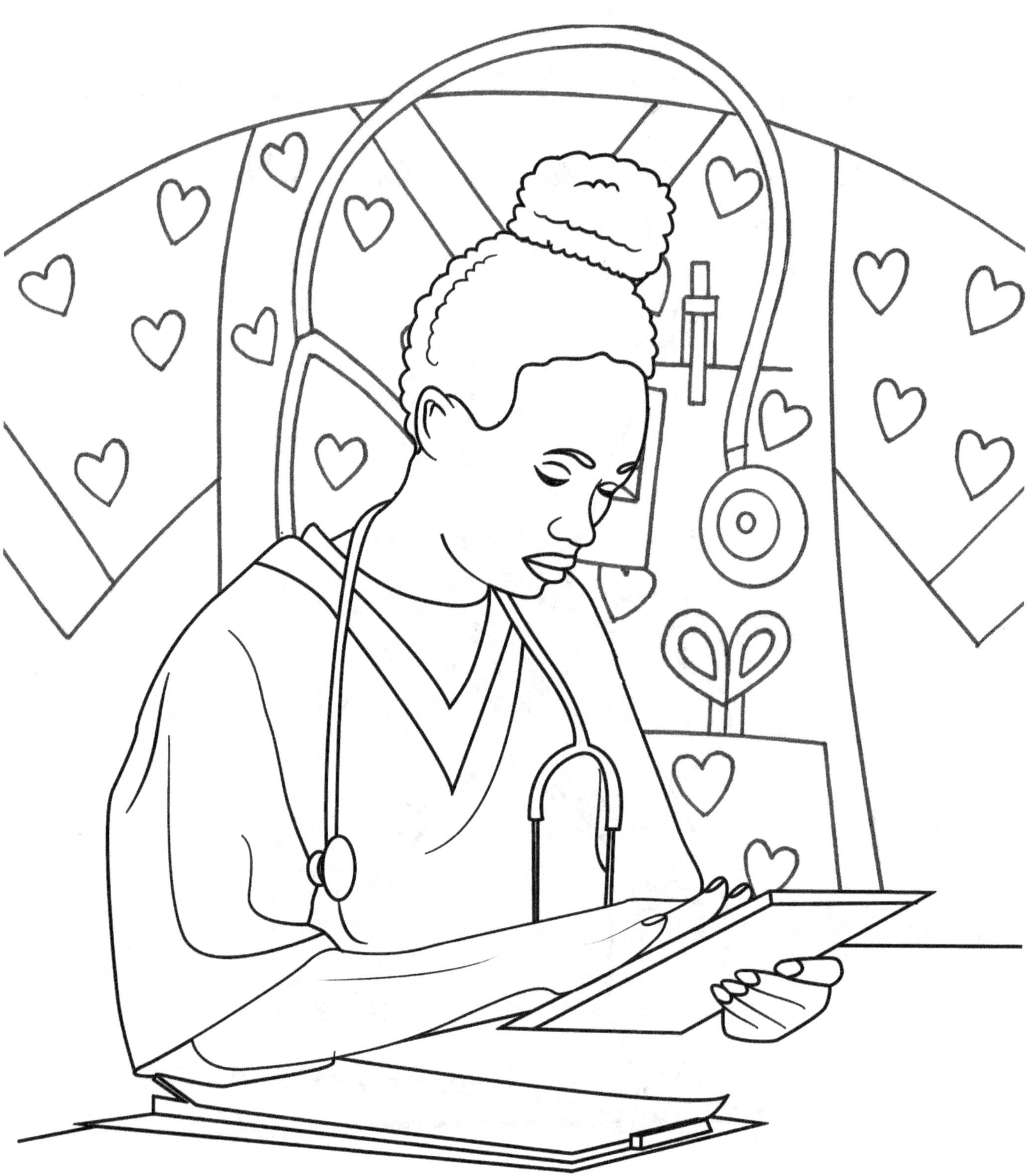

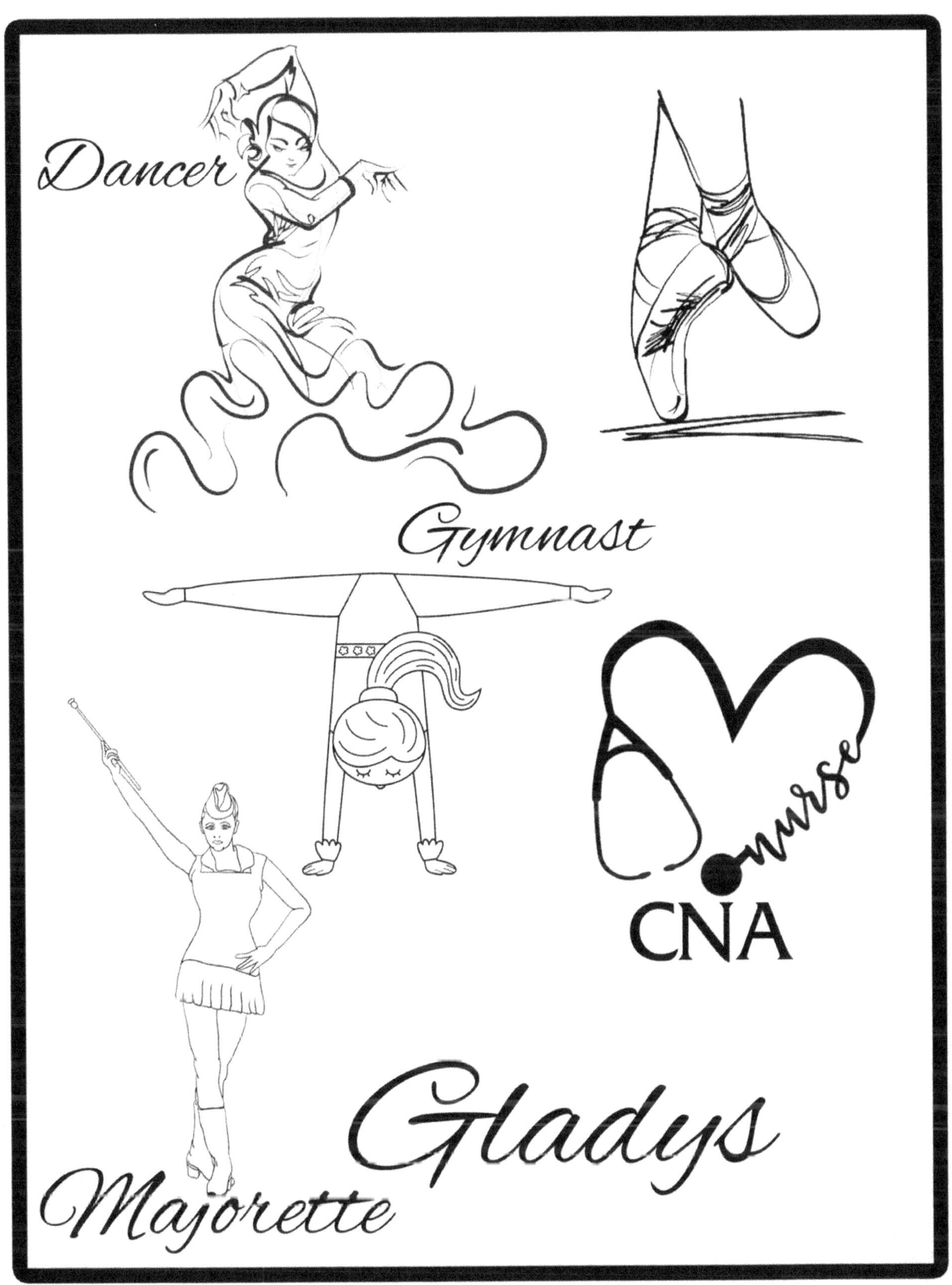
Dancer
Gymnast
nurse
CNA
Gladys
Majorette

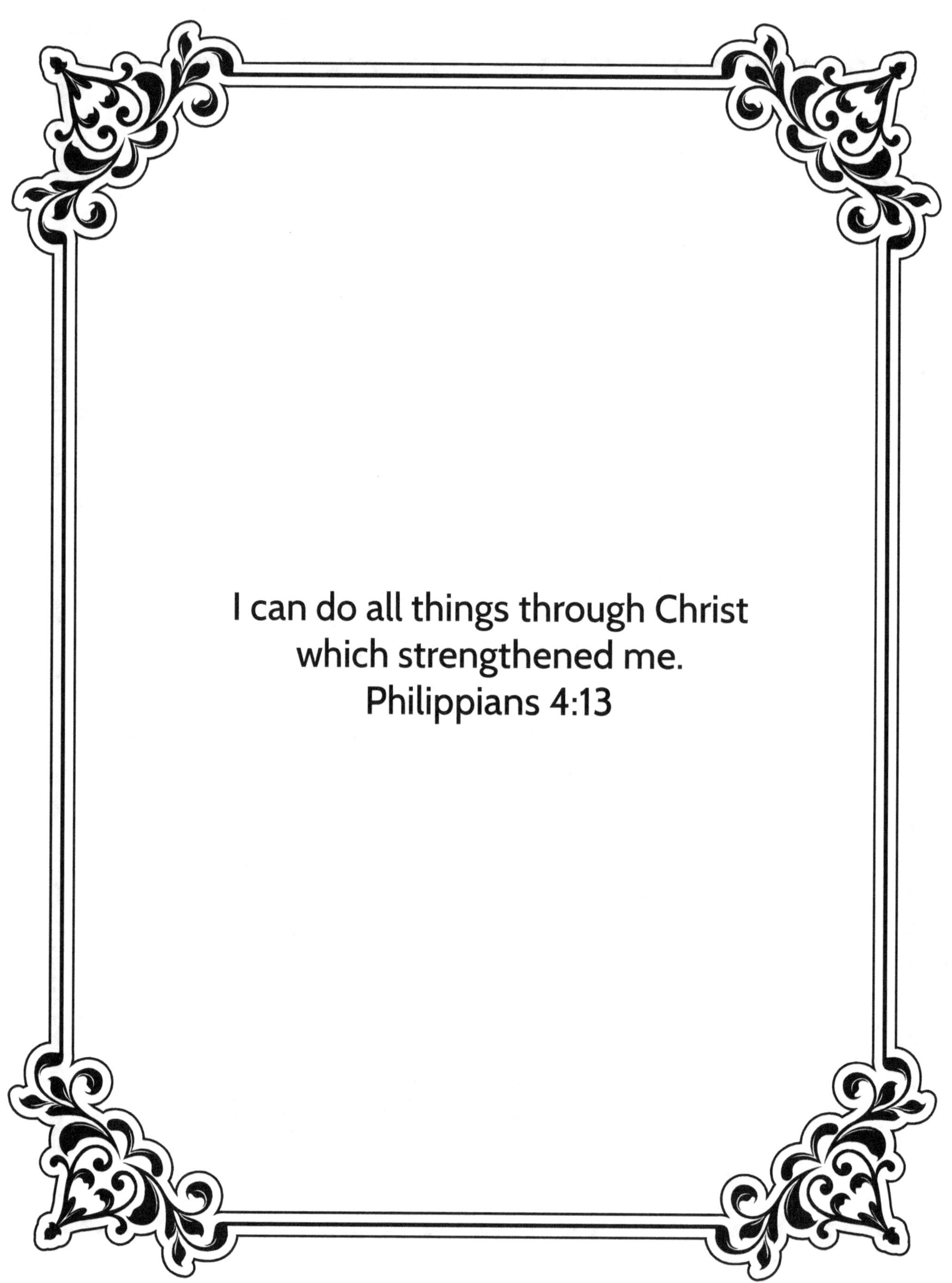
I can do all things through Christ
which strengthened me.
Philippians 4:13

Erma was a Dancer, Gymnast, and a Soloist

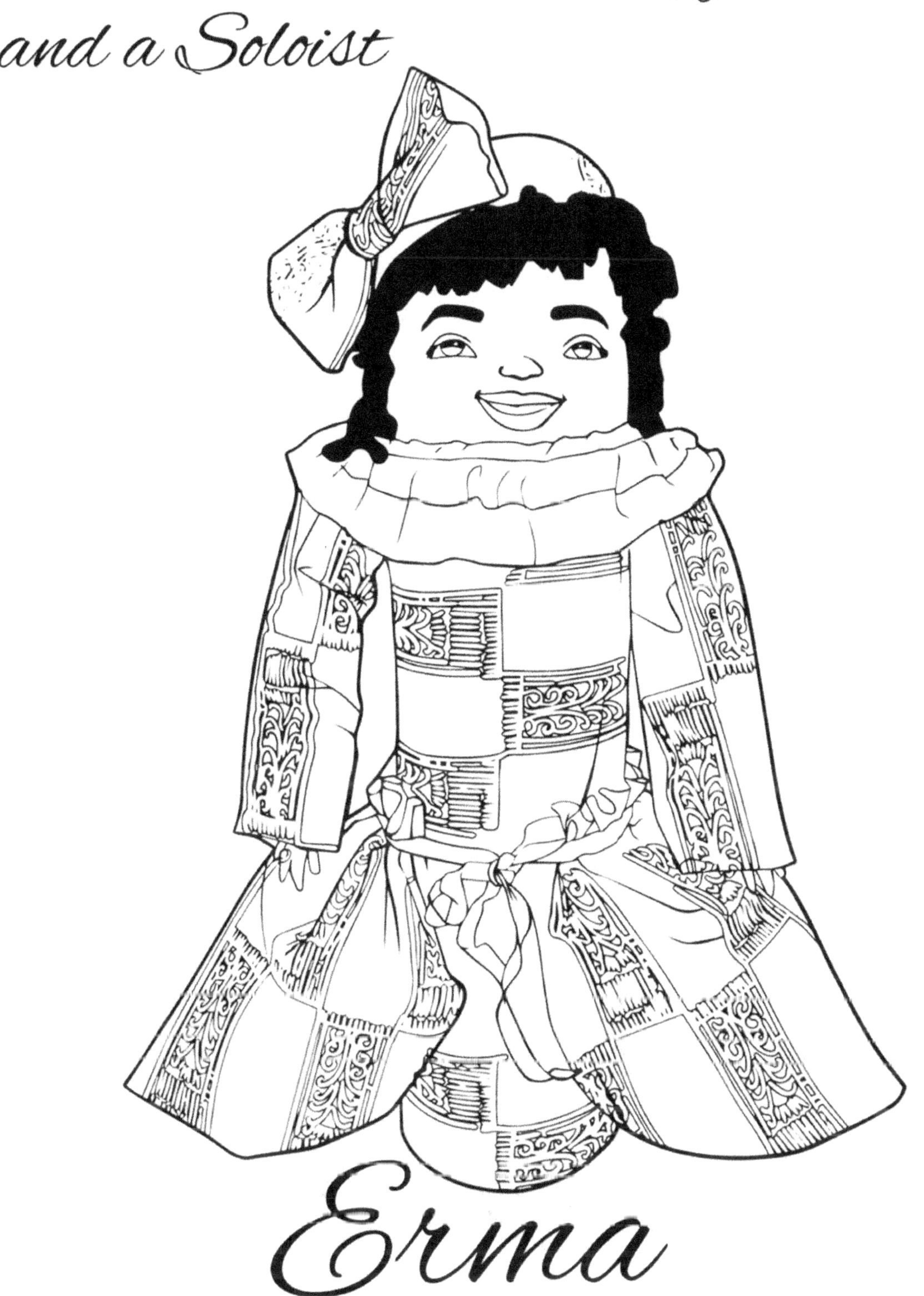

Erma

Luerine Madison Spencer

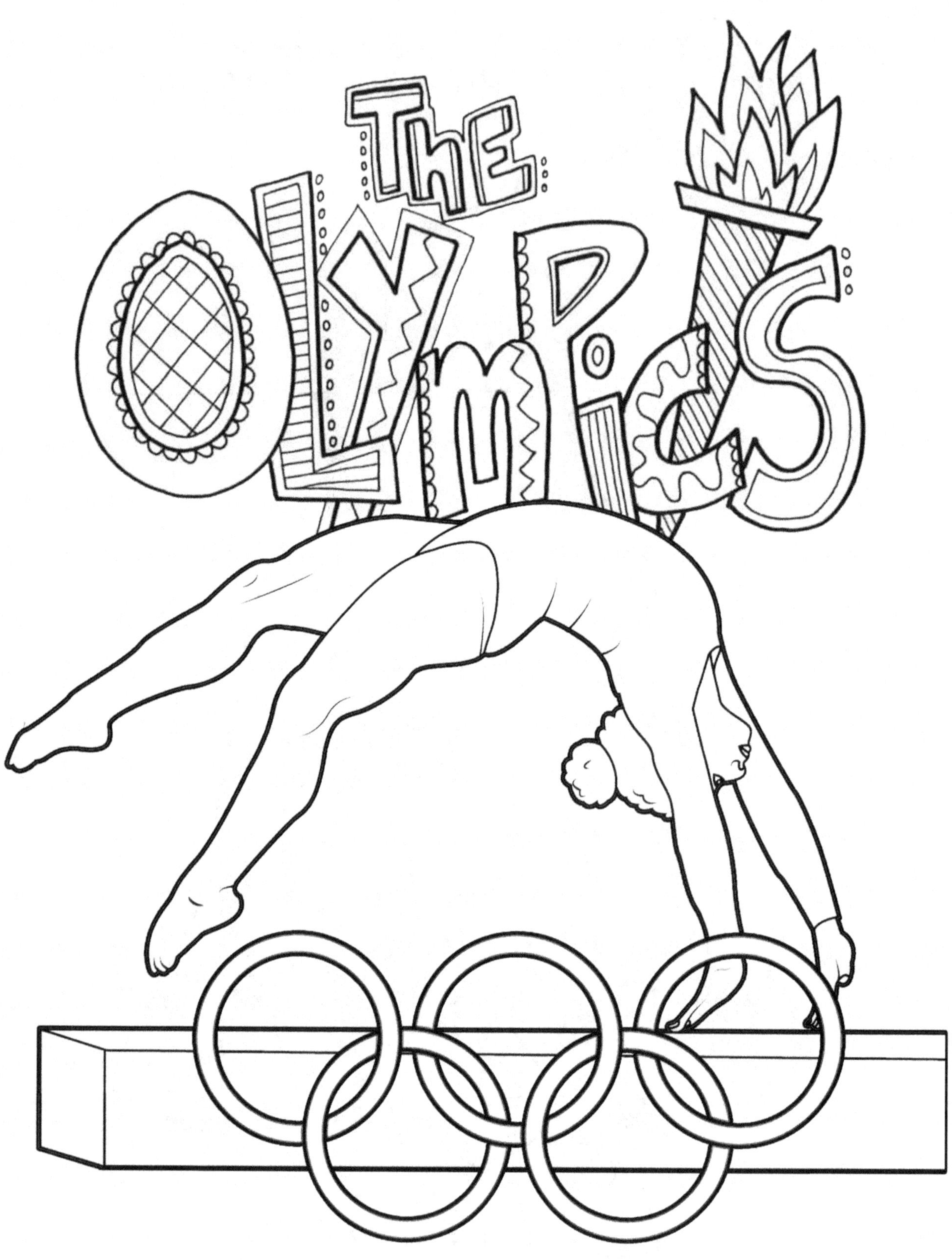

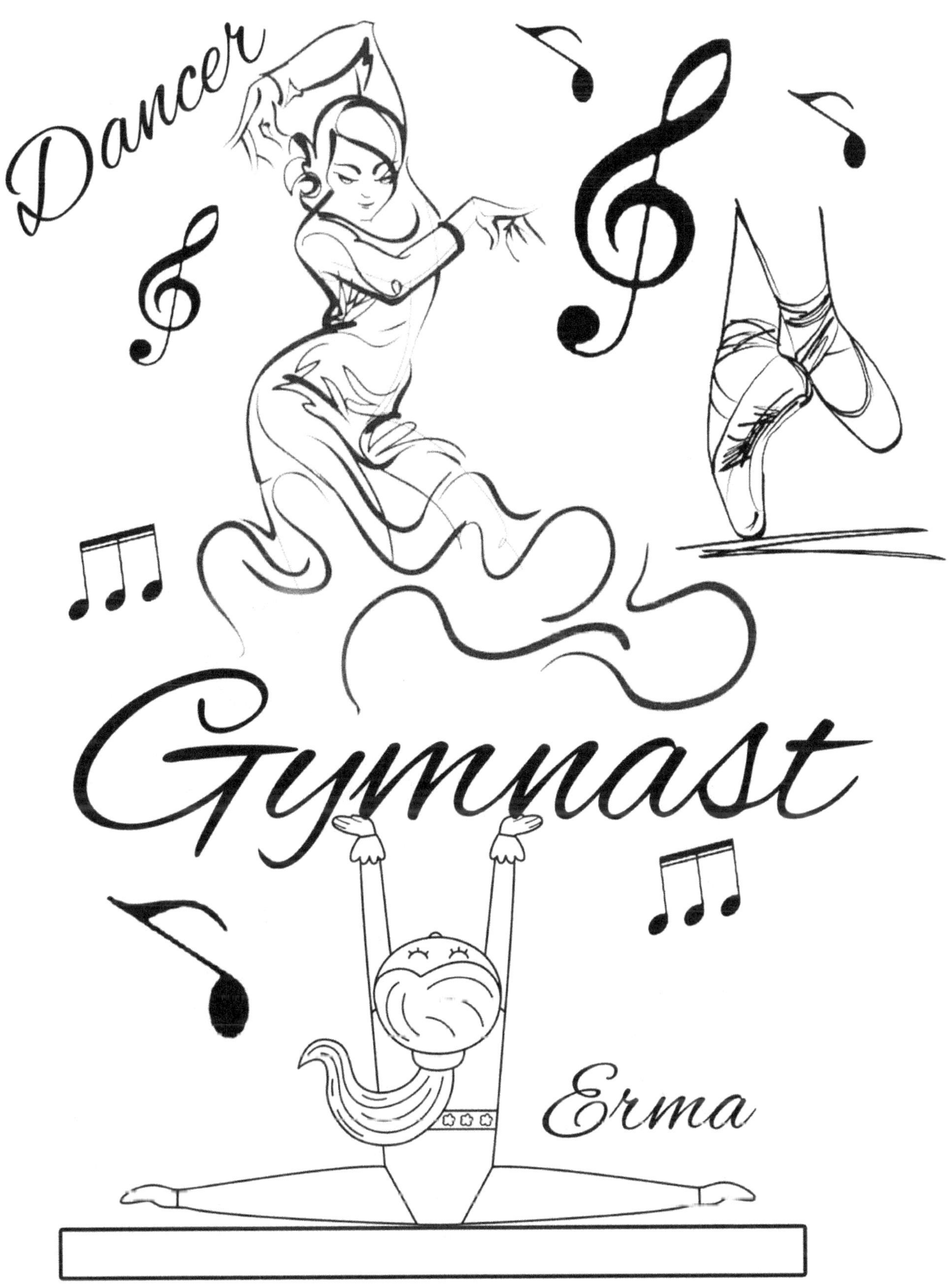
Dancer
Gymnast
Erma

Luerine Madison Spencer

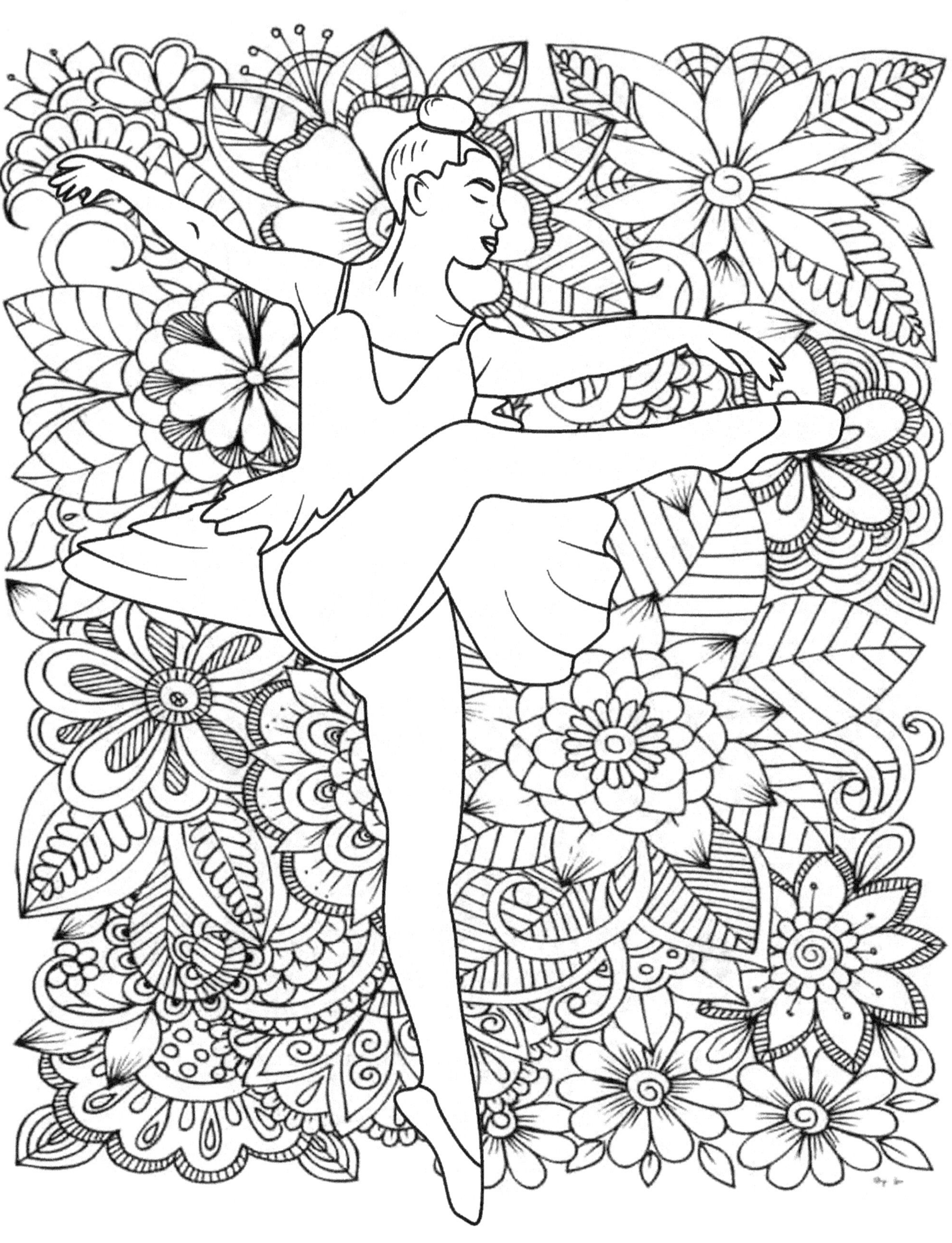

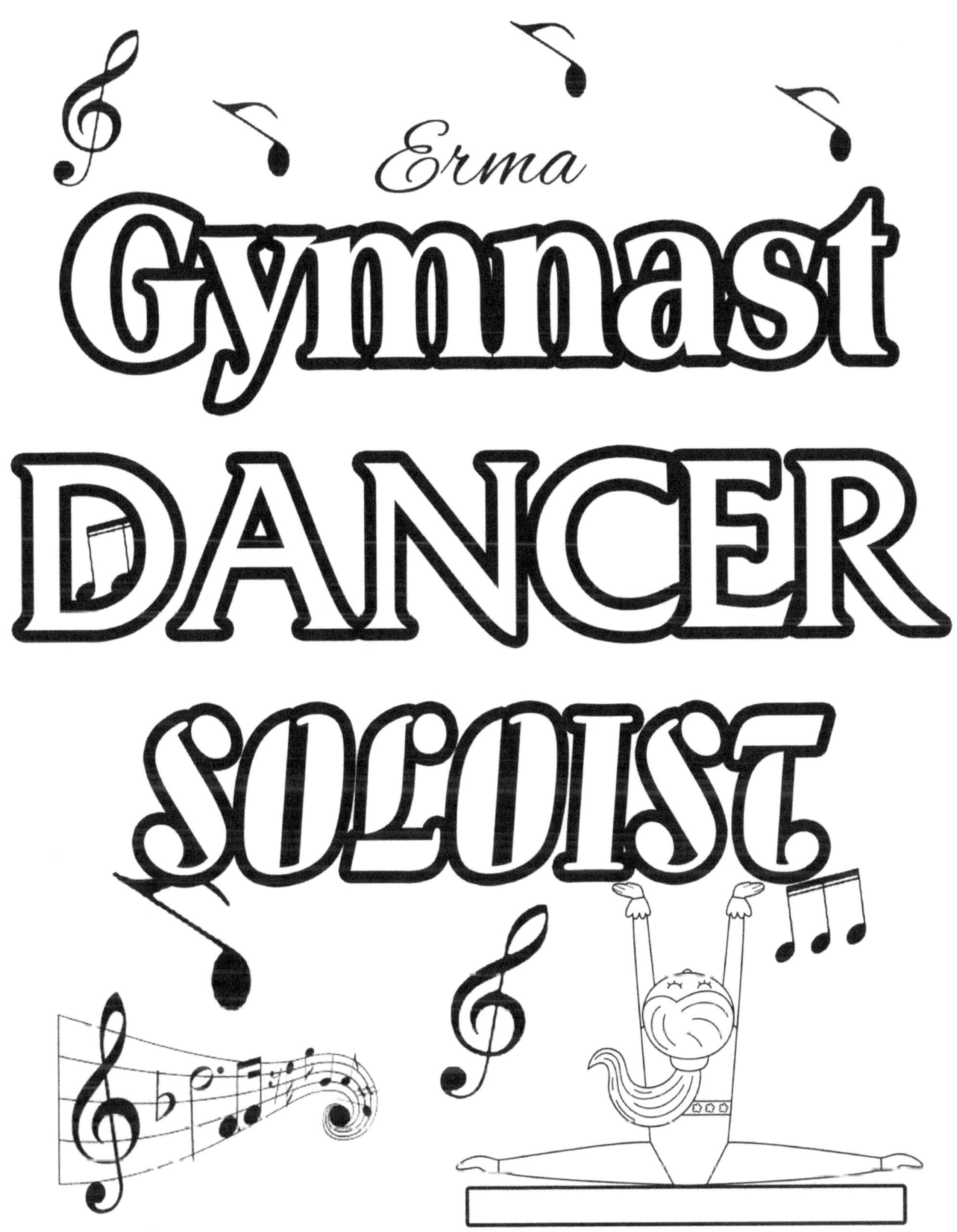

Erma
Gymnast
DANCER
SOLOIST

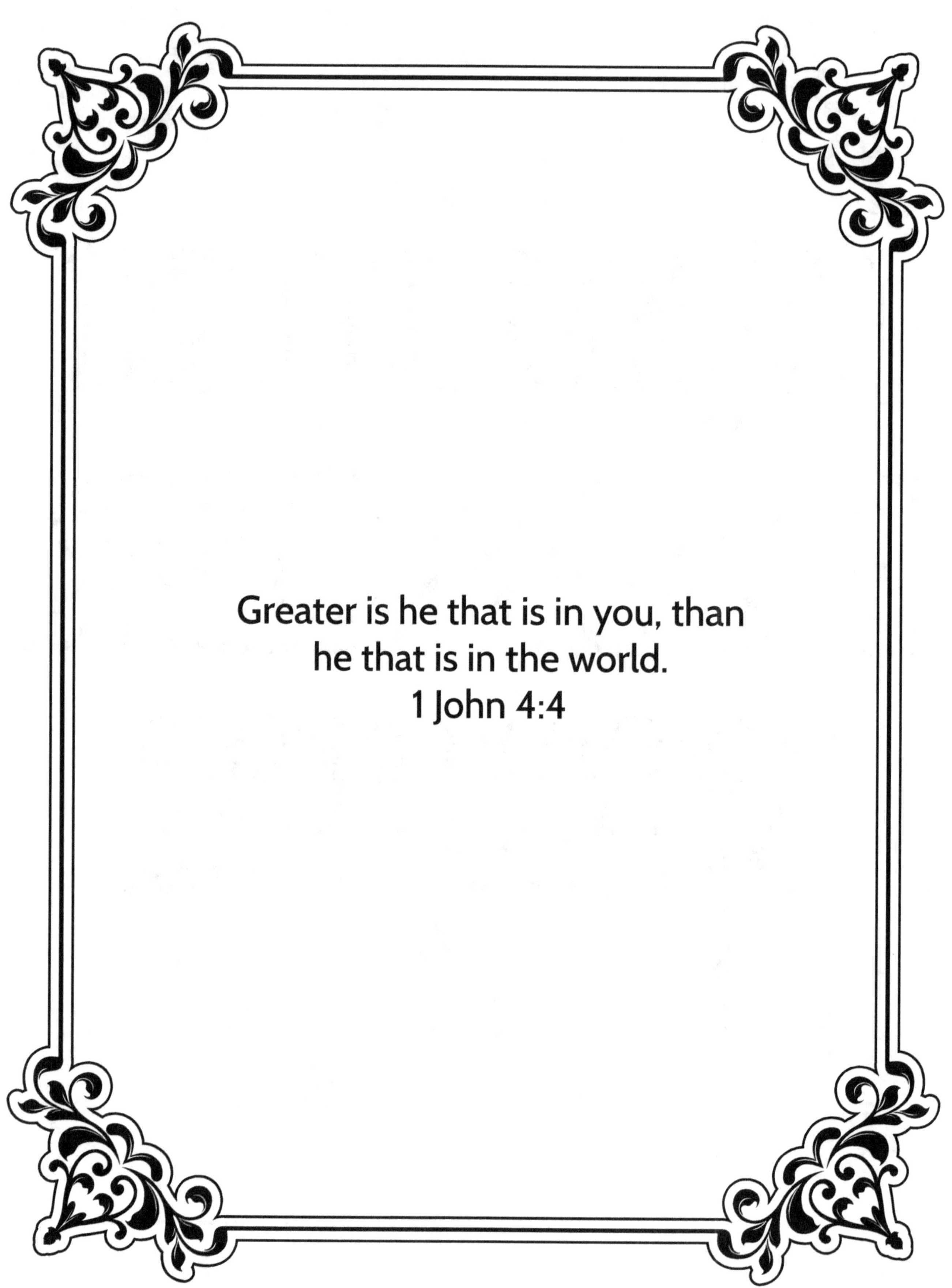

Greater is he that is in you, than
he that is in the world.
1 John 4:4

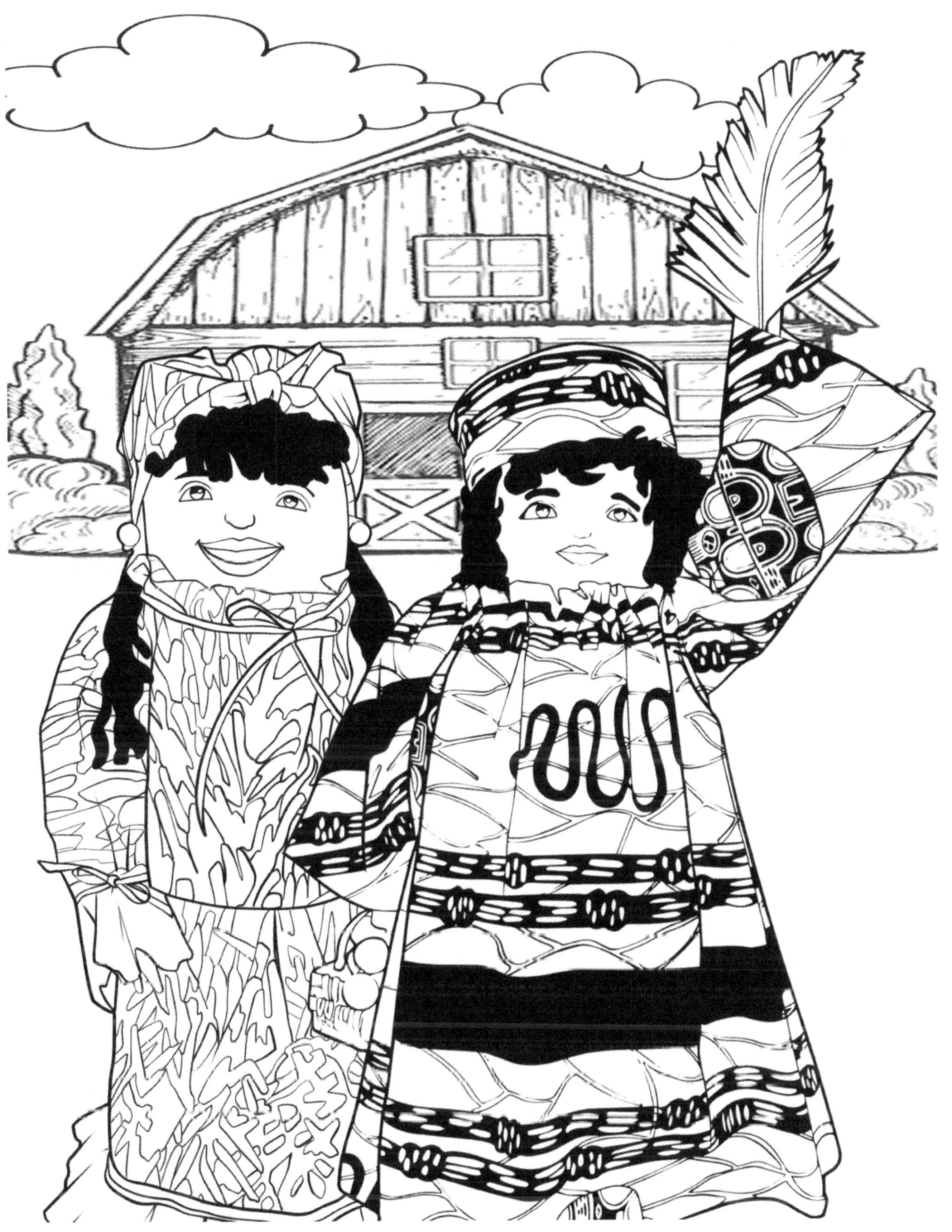

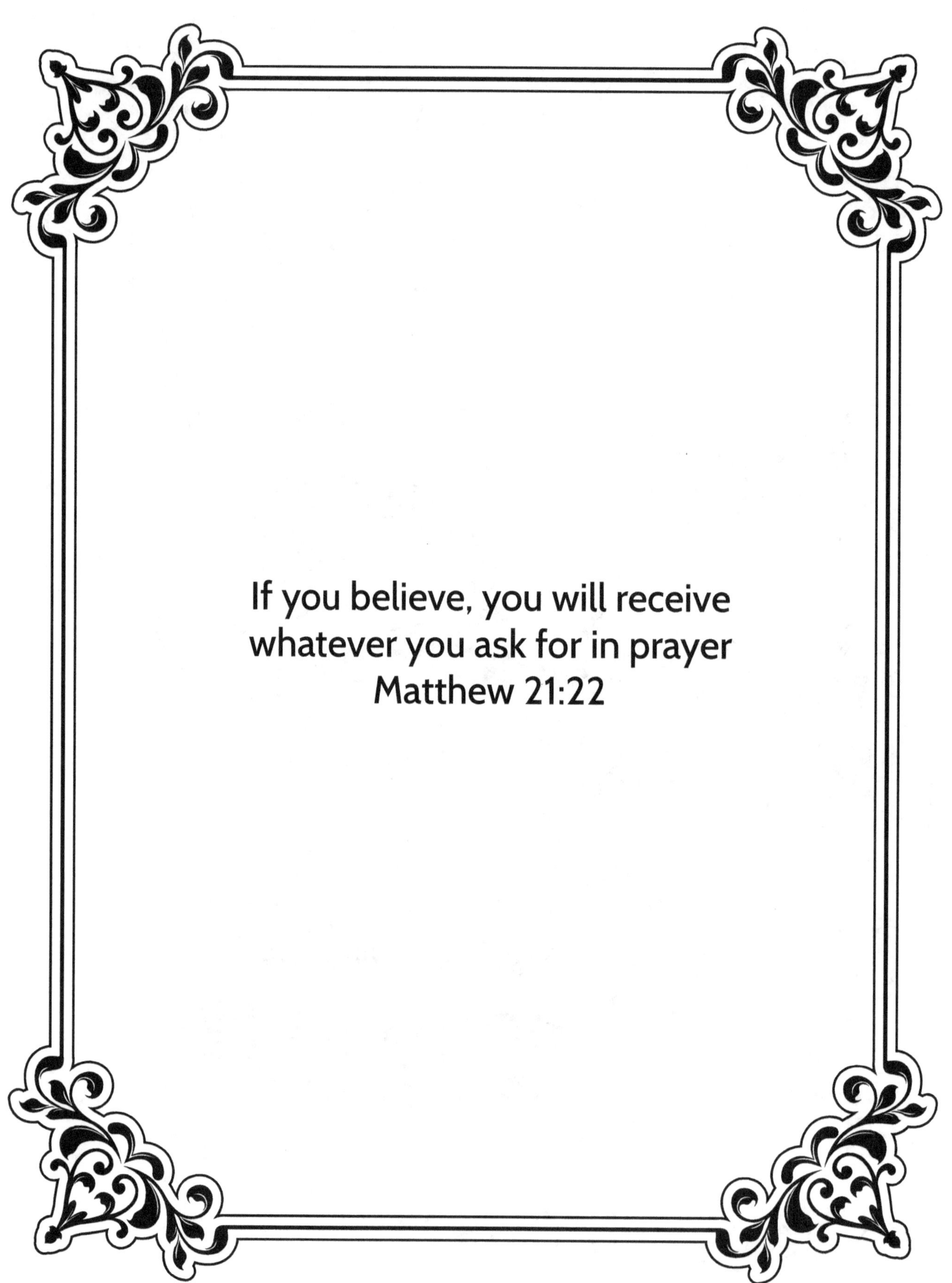

Luerine Madison Spencer

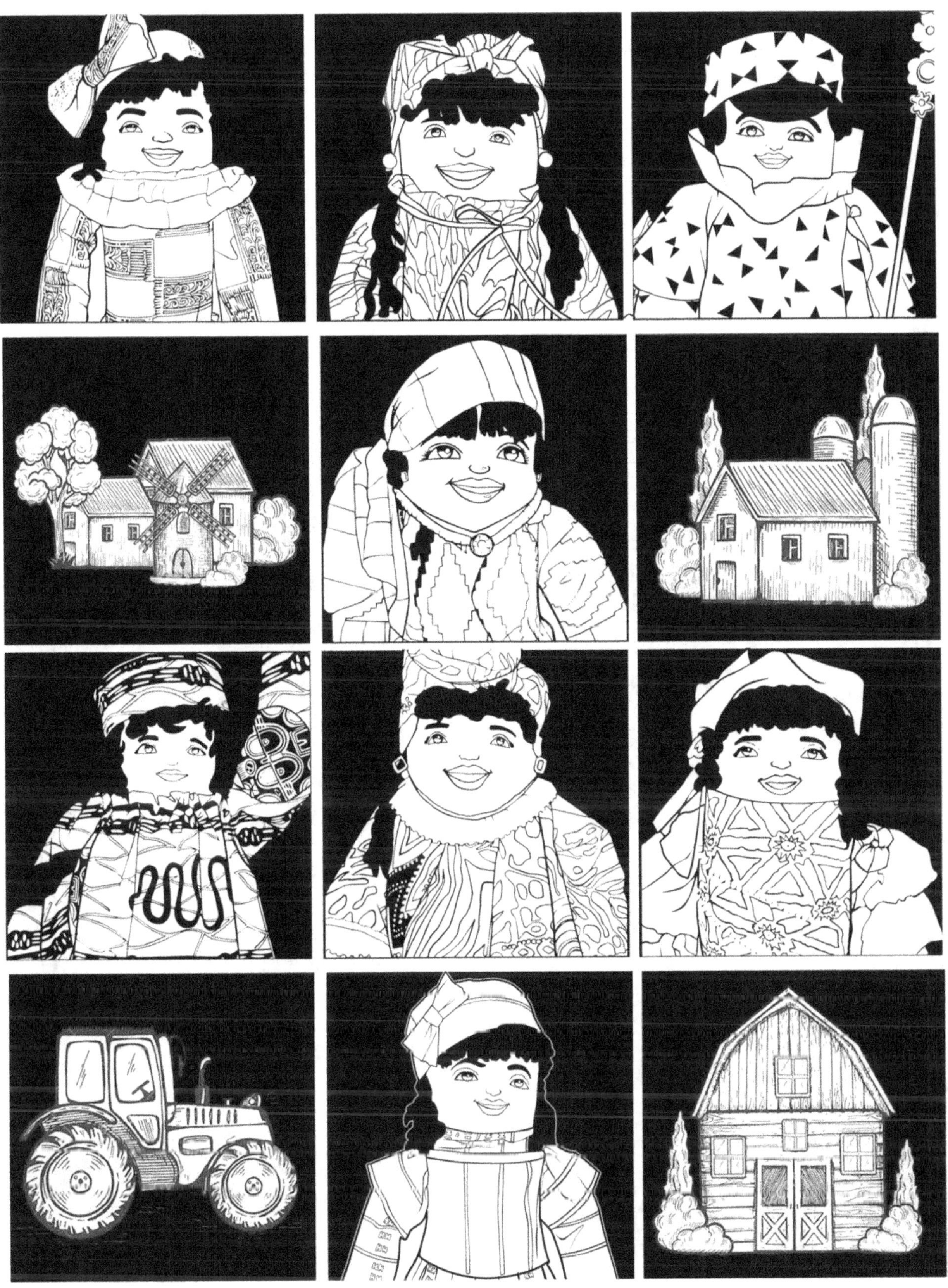

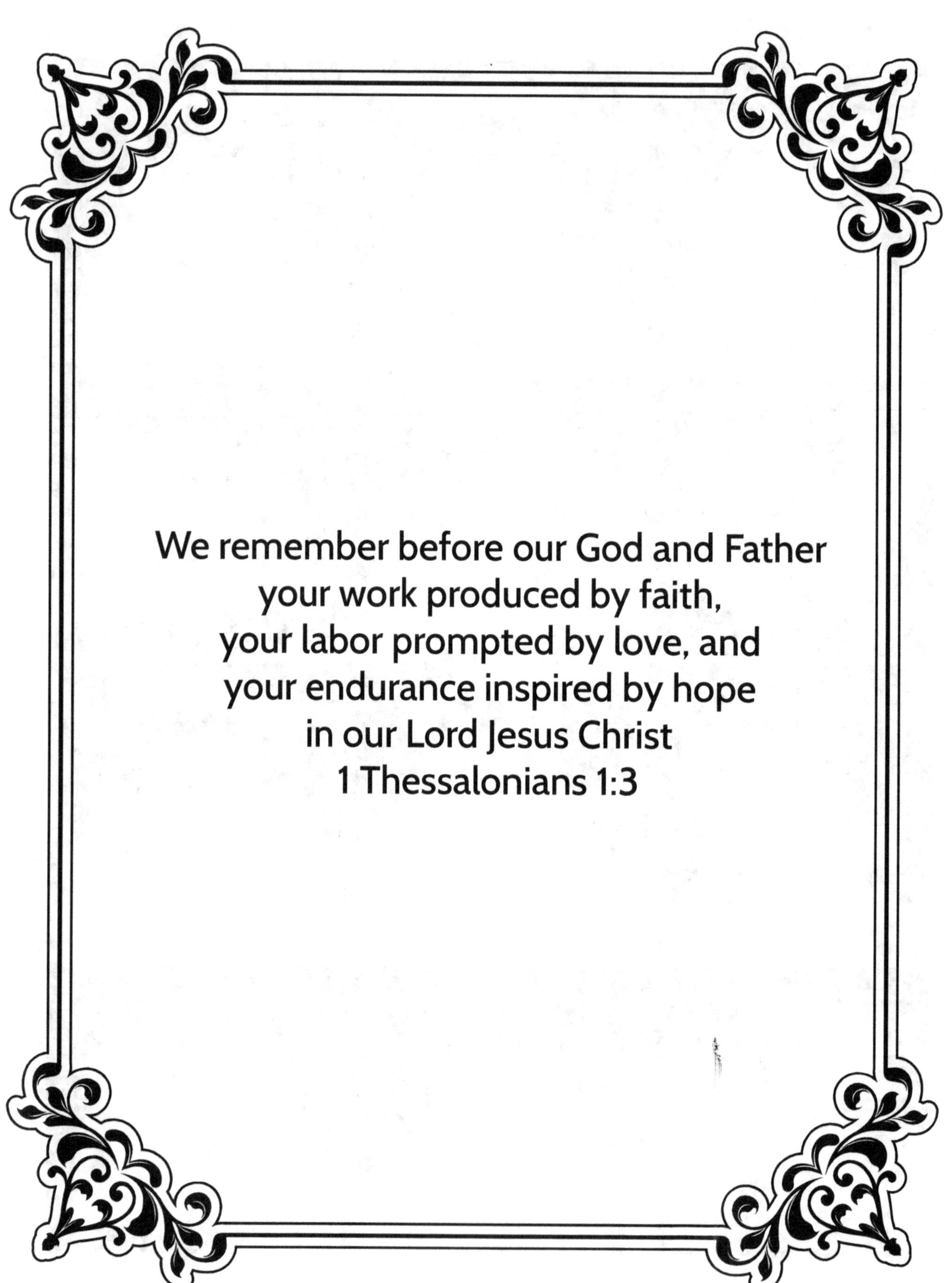

We remember before our God and Father
your work produced by faith,
your labor prompted by love, and
your endurance inspired by hope
in our Lord Jesus Christ
1 Thessalonians 1:3

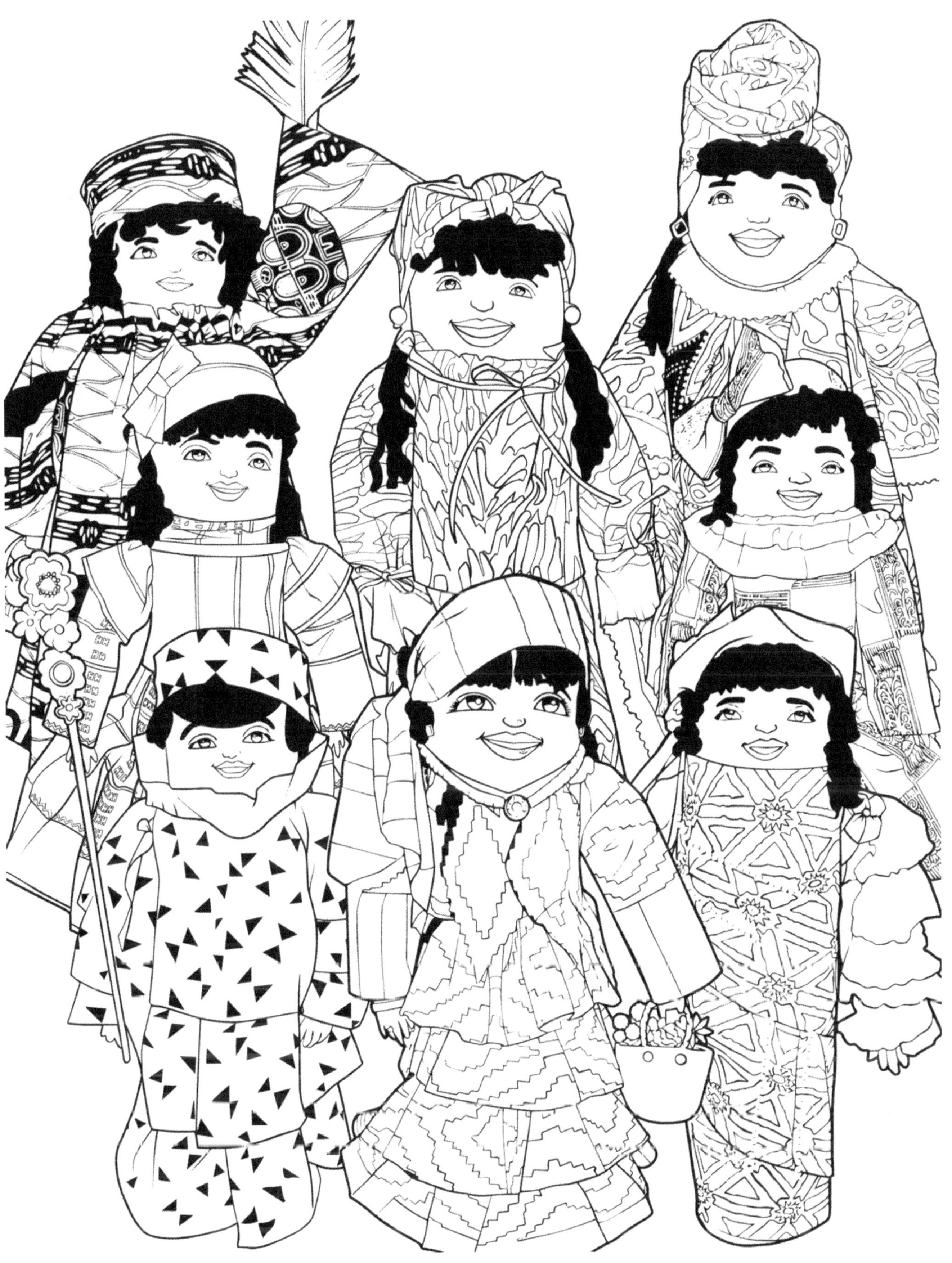

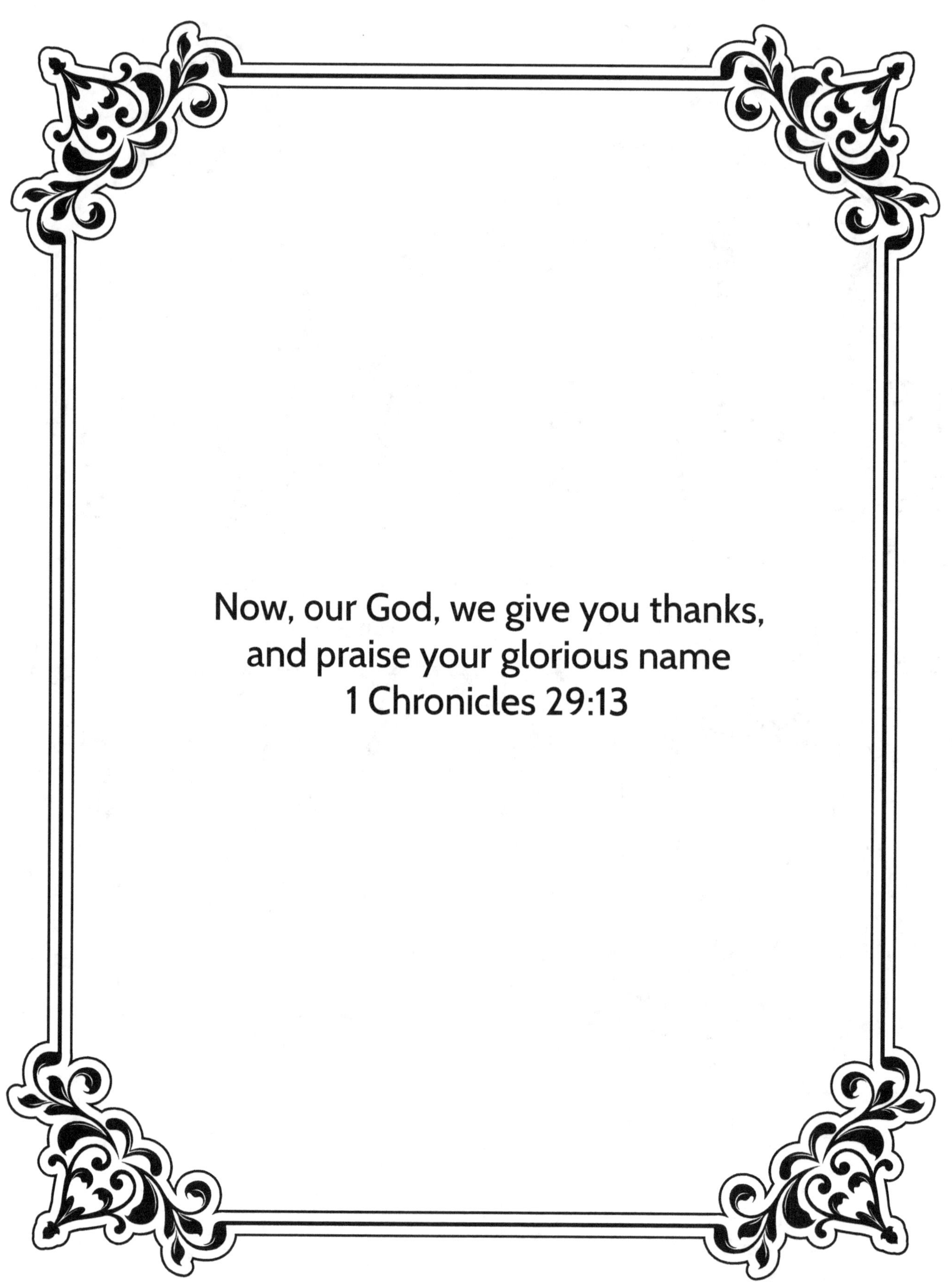

Now, our God, we give you thanks,
and praise your glorious name
1 Chronicles 29:13

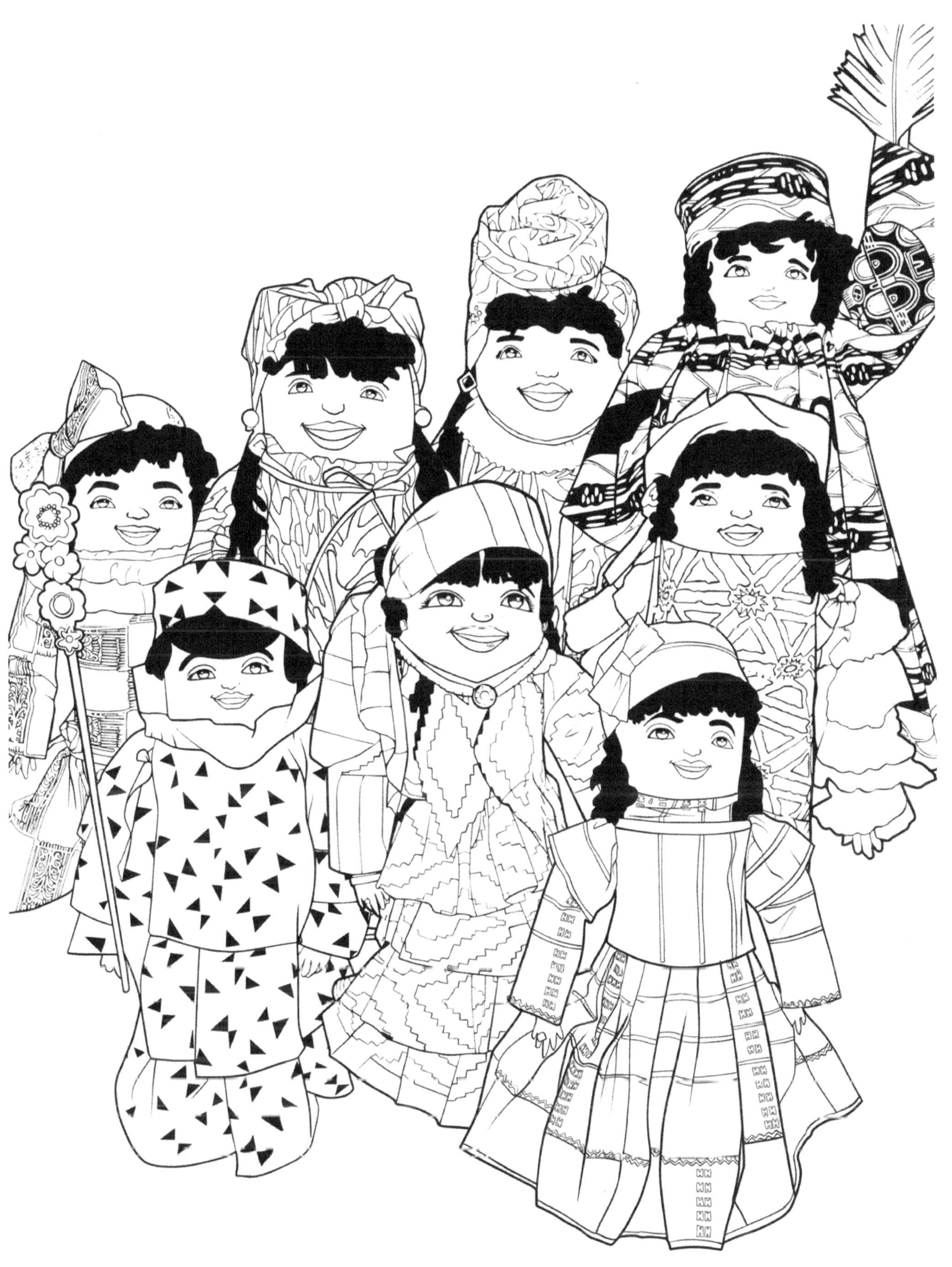

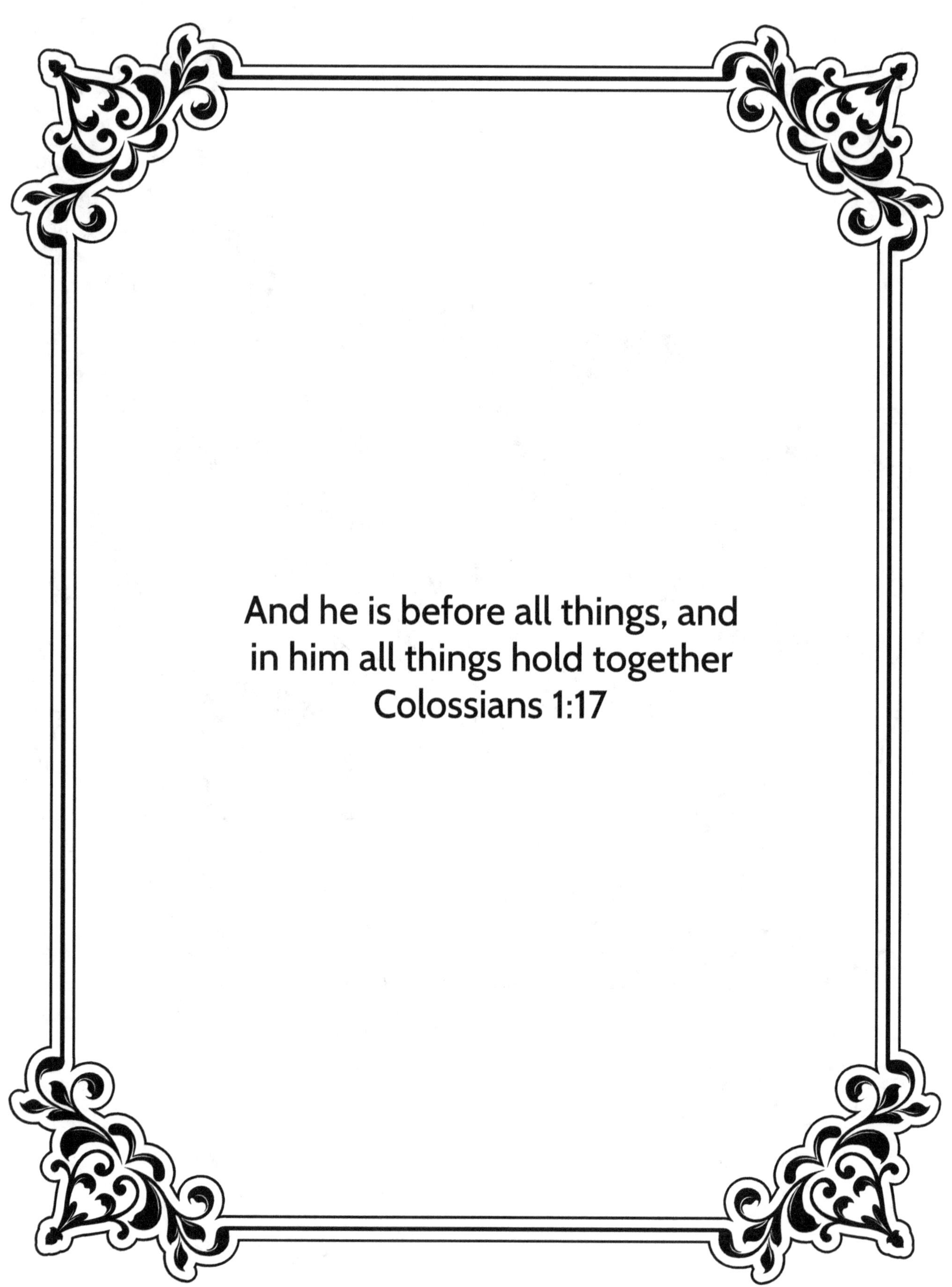

And he is before all things, and
in him all things hold together
Colossians 1:17

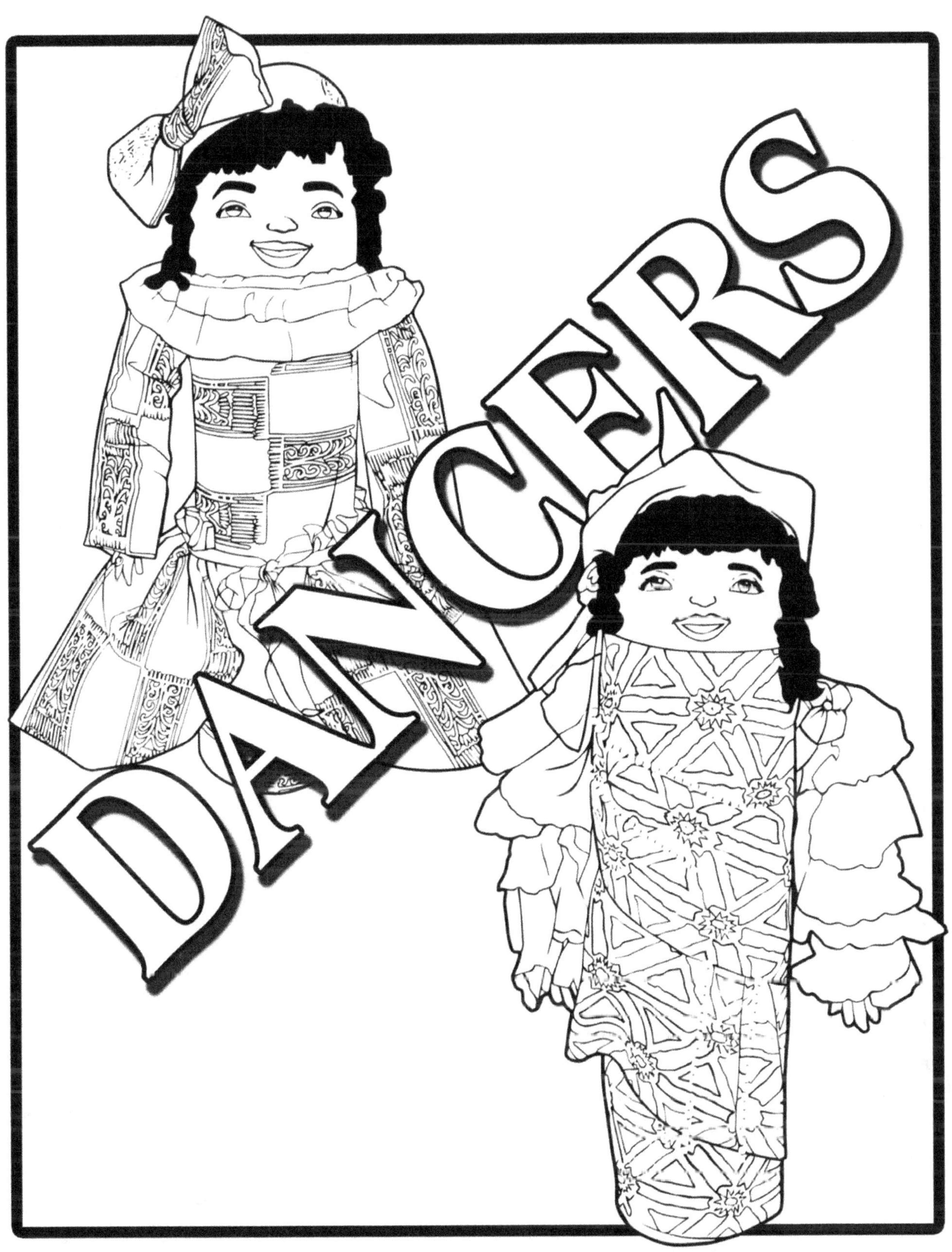
DANCERS

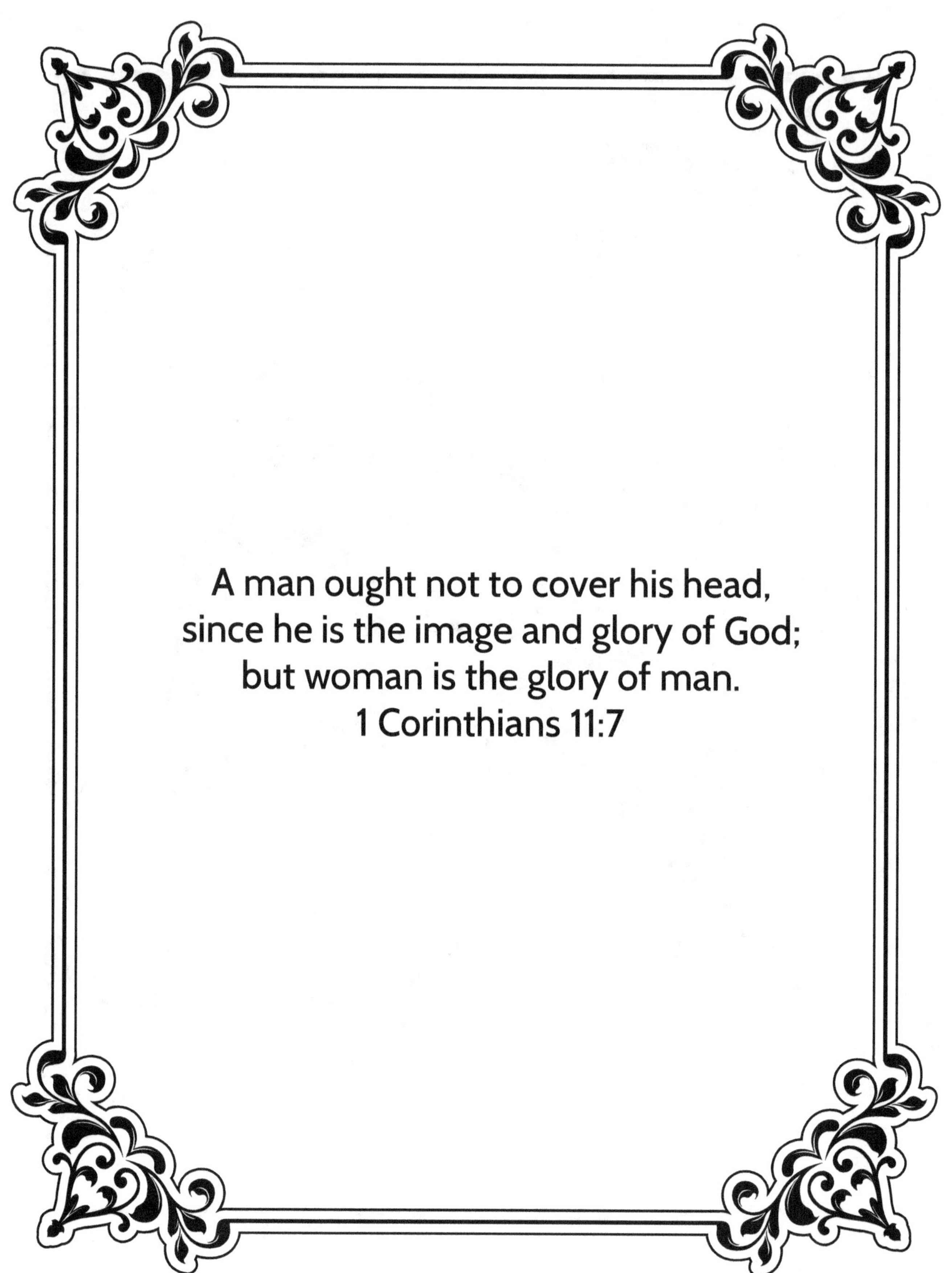

A man ought not to cover his head,
since he is the image and glory of God;
but woman is the glory of man.
1 Corinthians 11:7

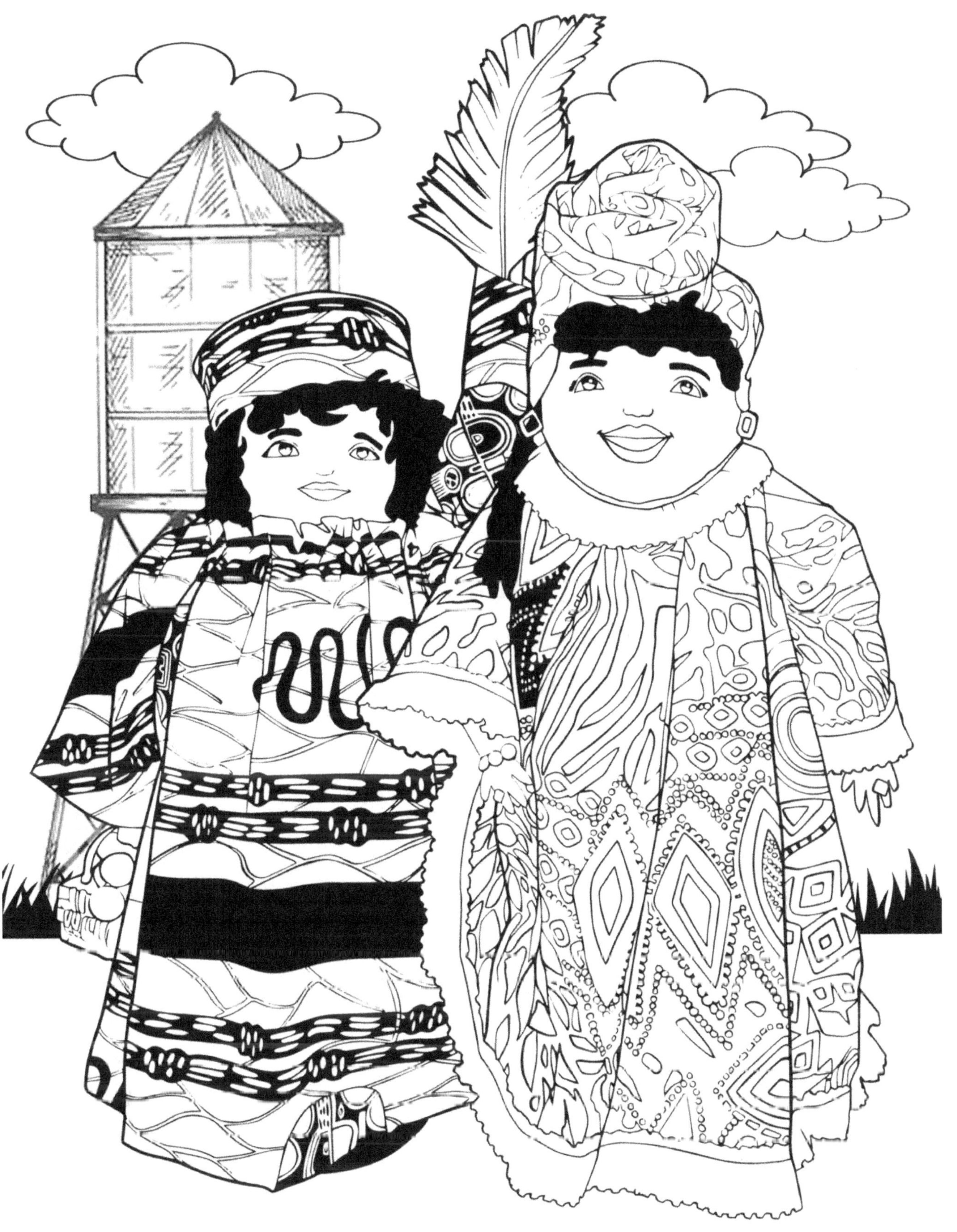

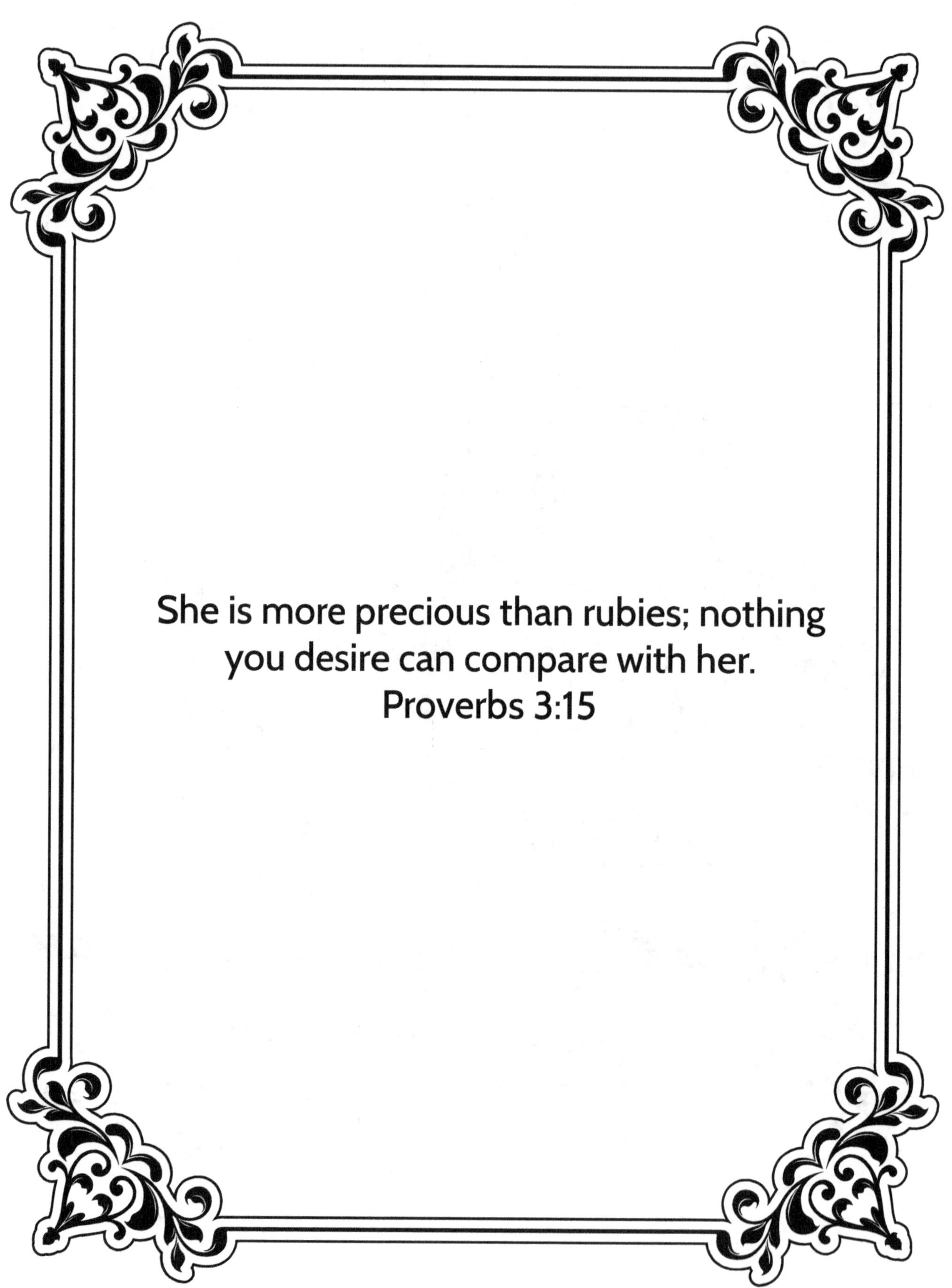
She is more precious than rubies; nothing
you desire can compare with her.
Proverbs 3:15

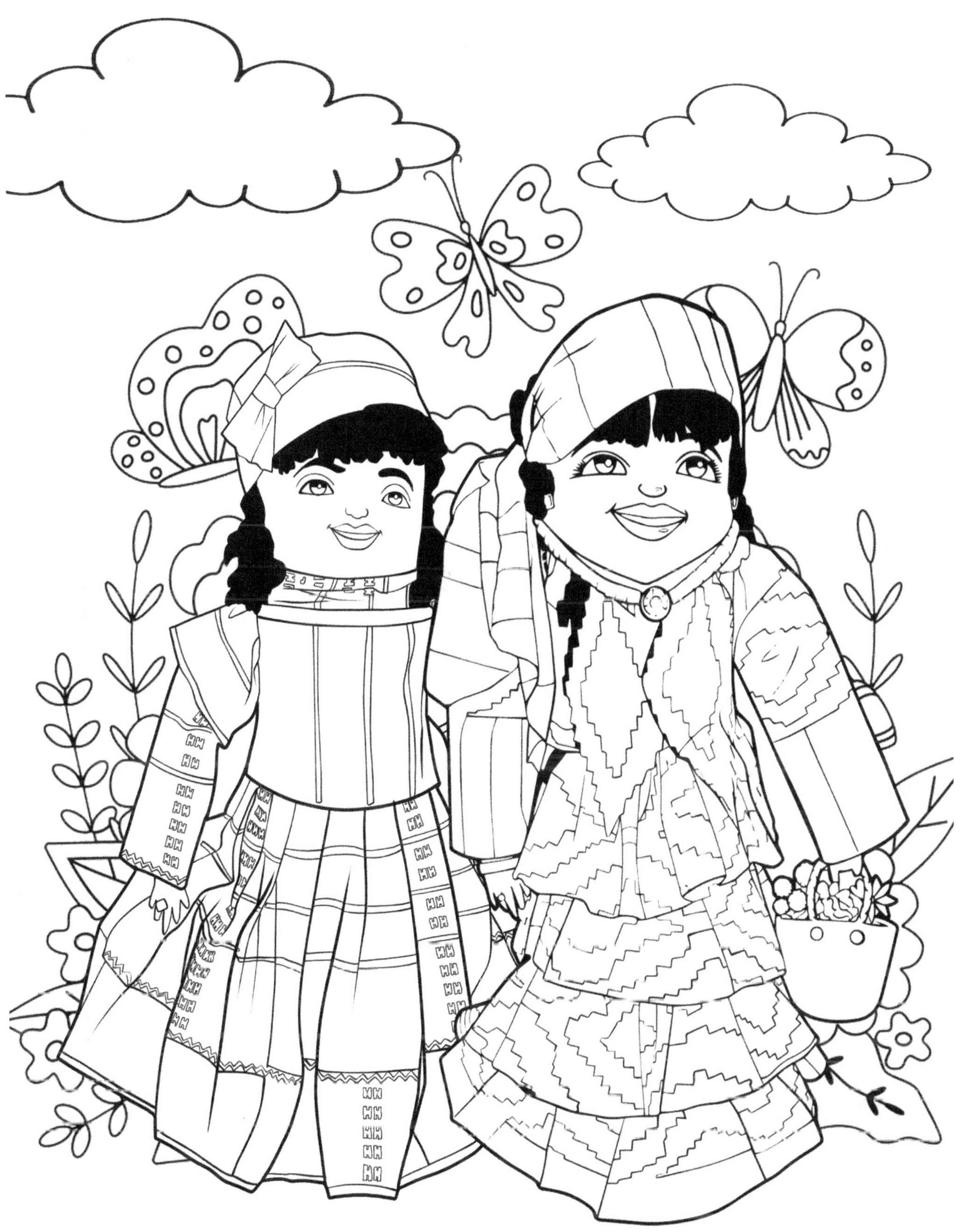

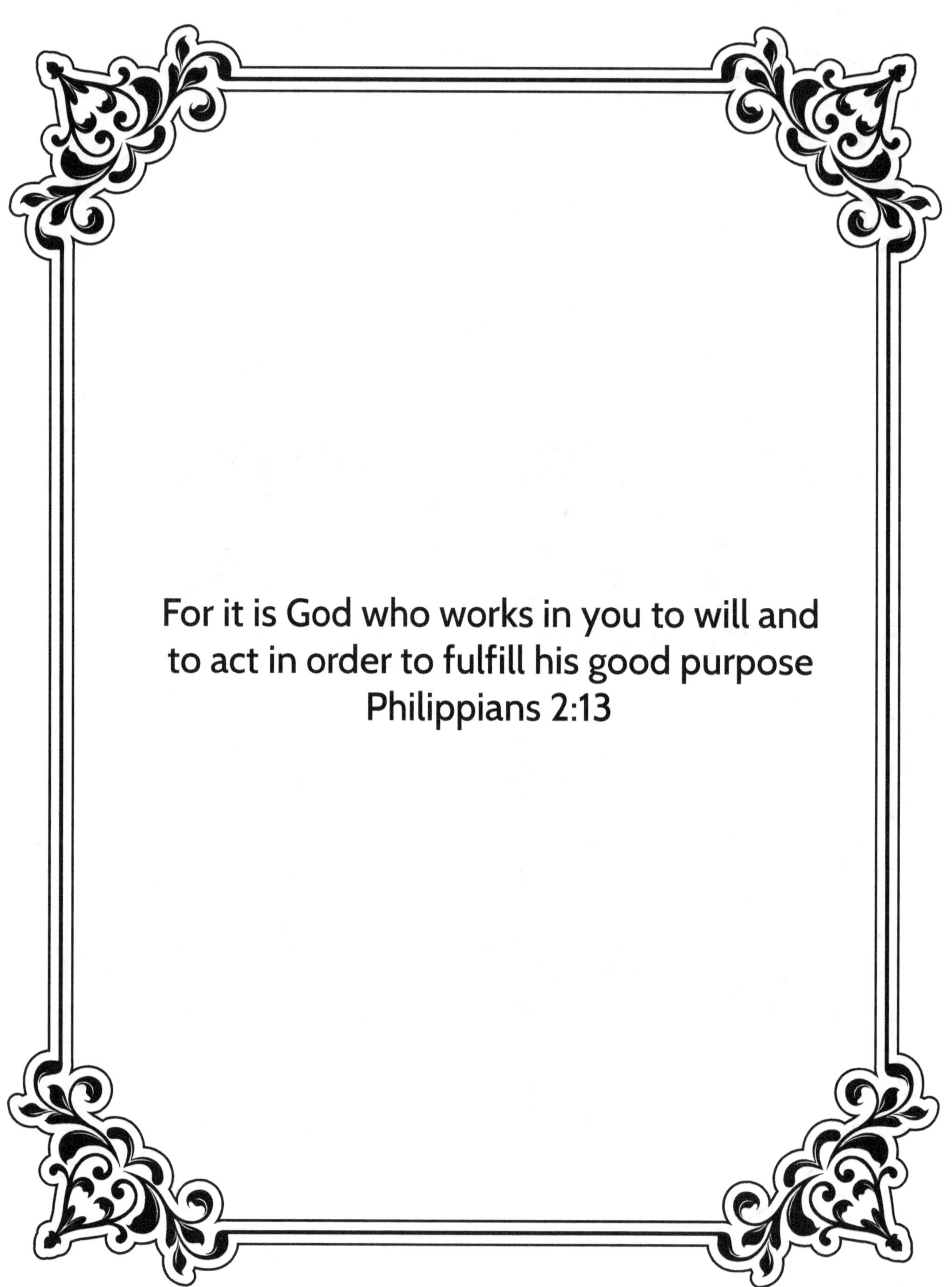
For it is God who works in you to will and
to act in order to fulfill his good purpose
Philippians 2:13

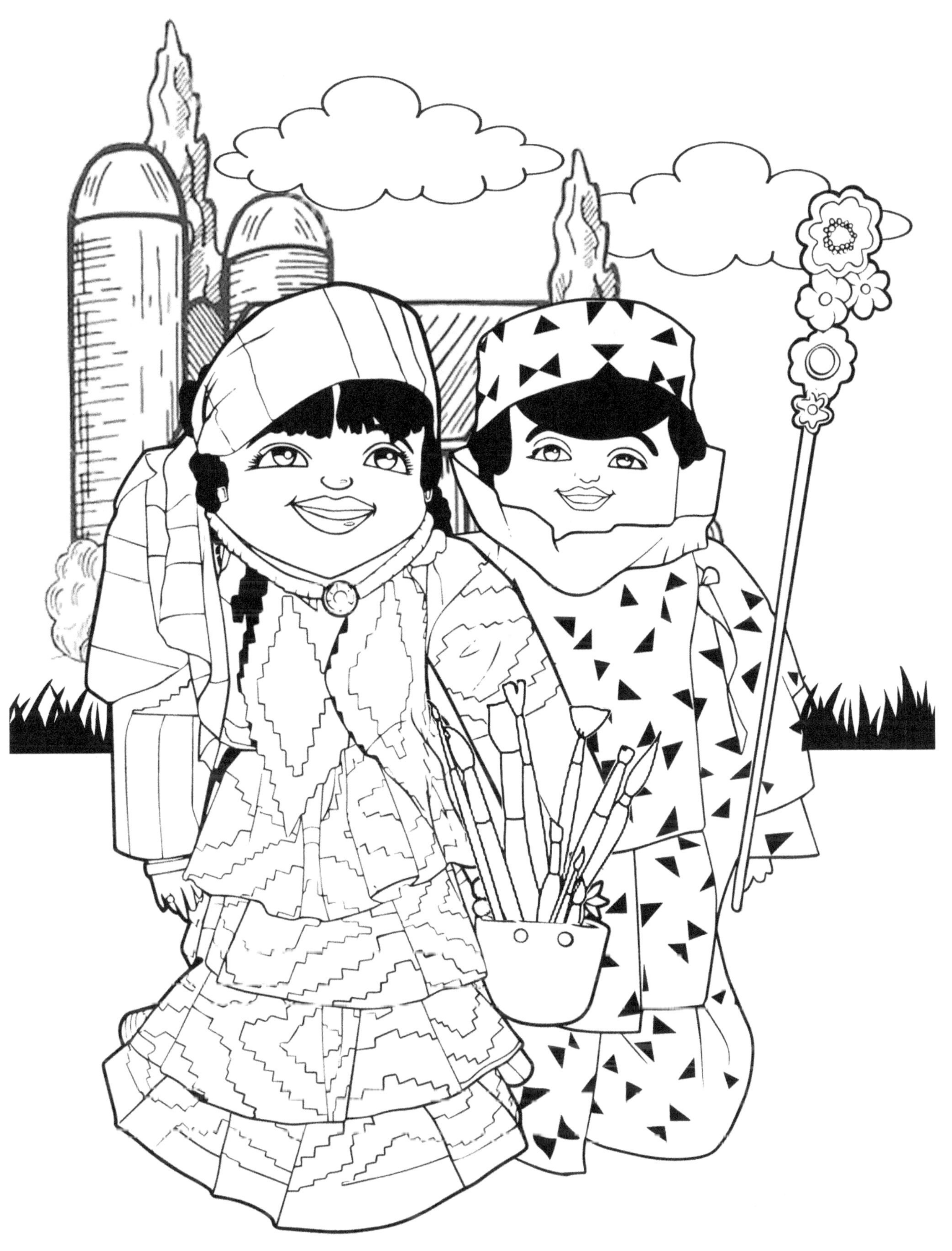

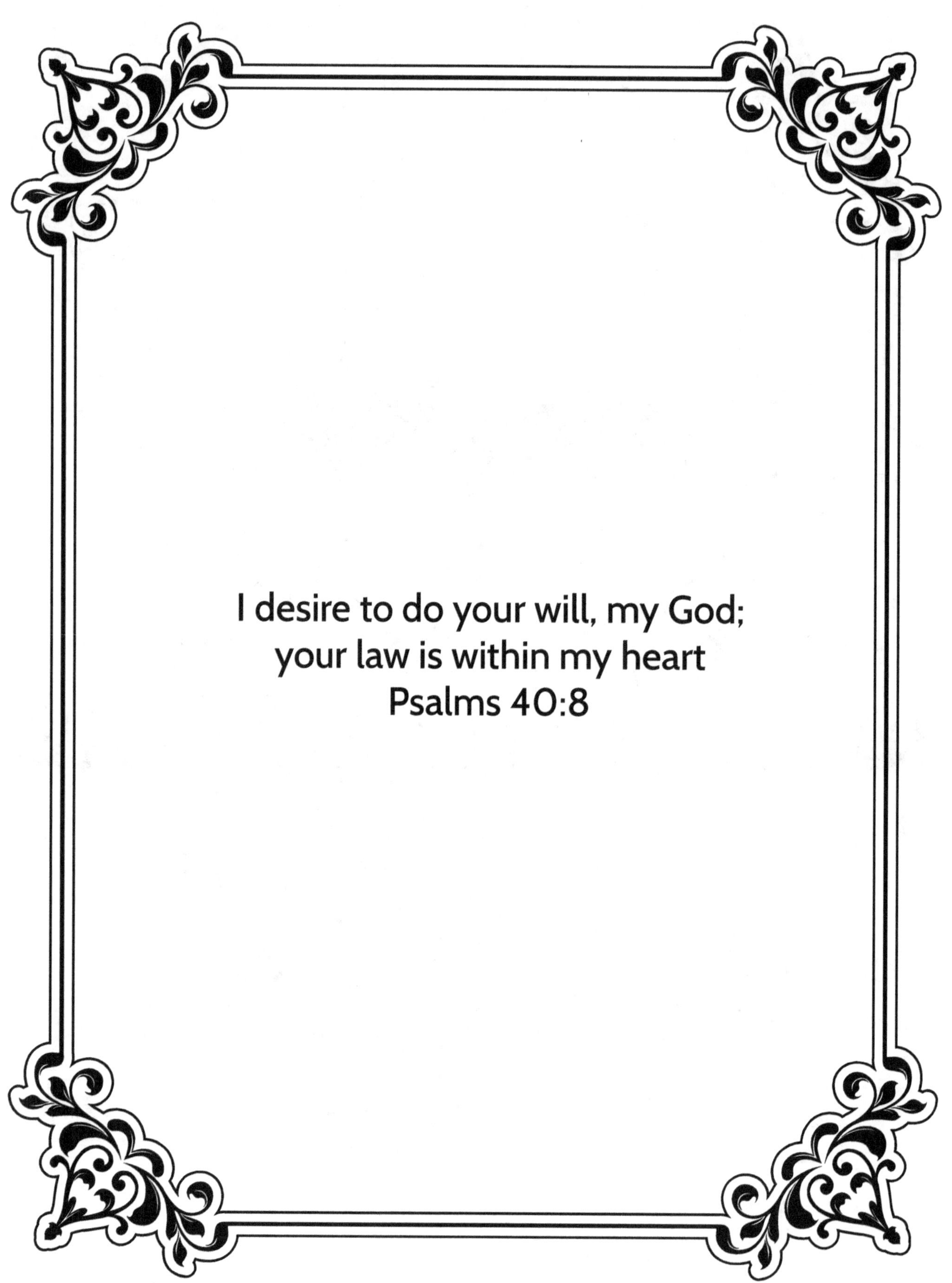
Luerine Madison Spencer
I desire to do your will, my God;
your law is within my heart
Psalms 40:8

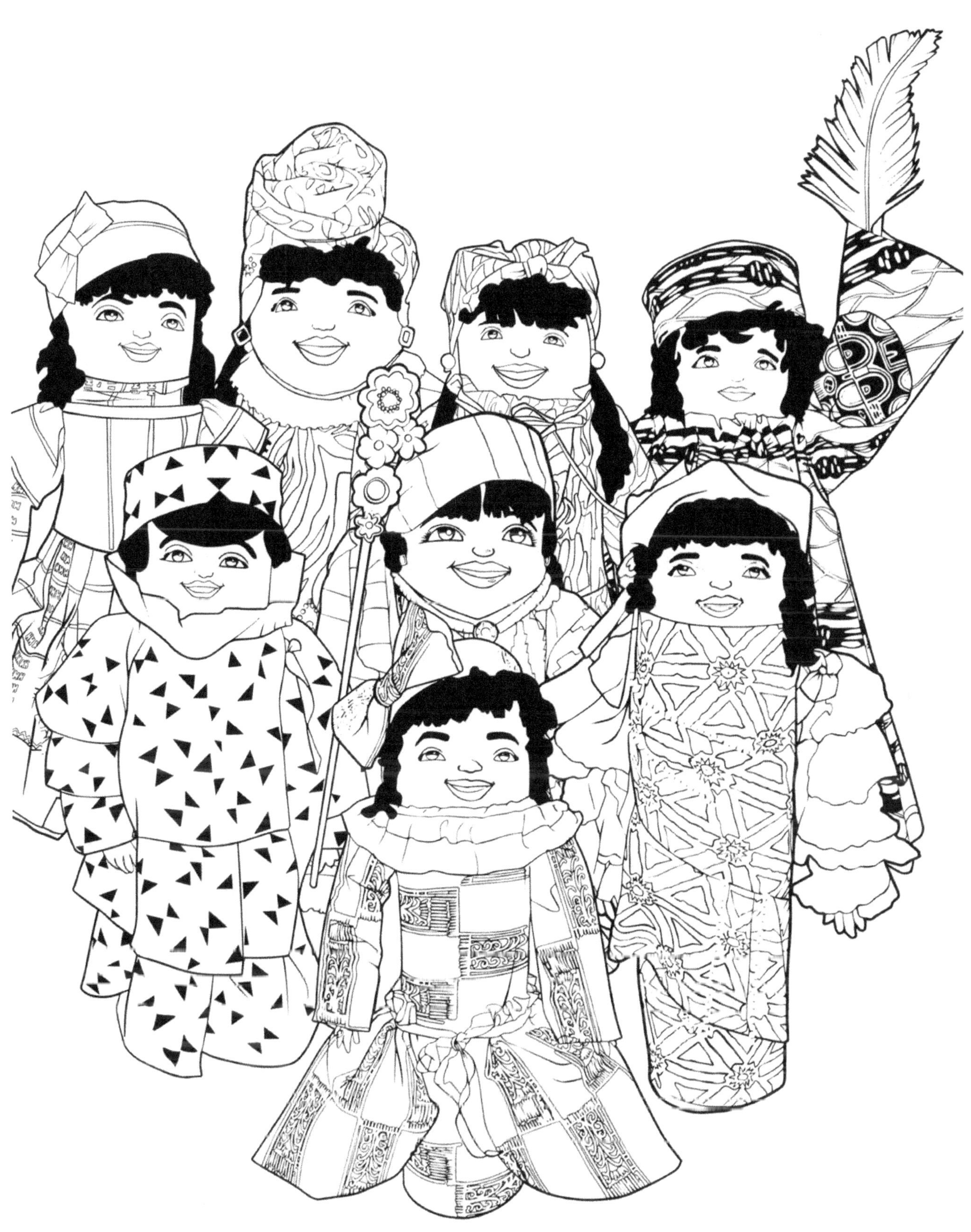

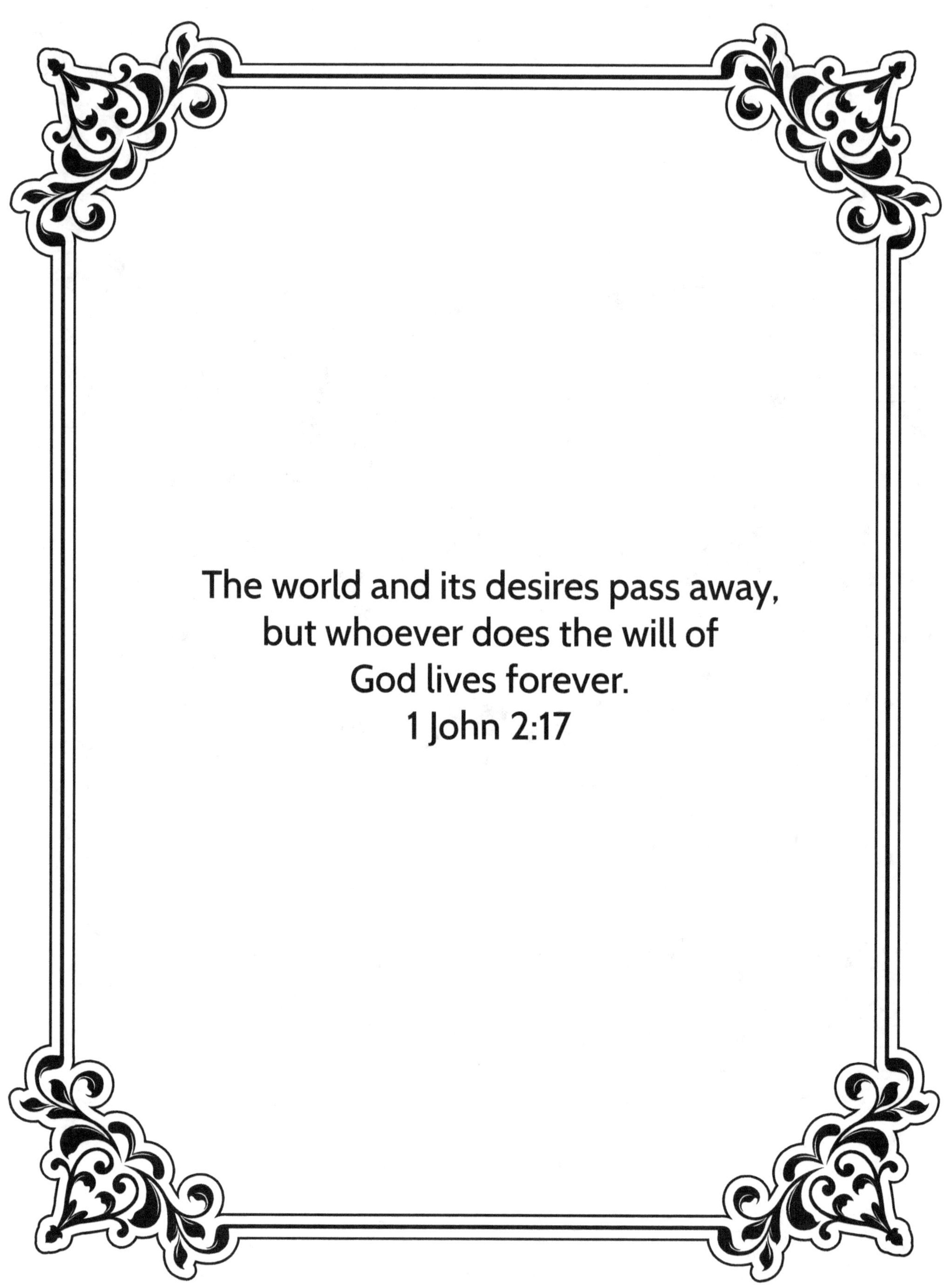

The world and its desires pass away,
but whoever does the will of
God lives forever.
1 John 2:17

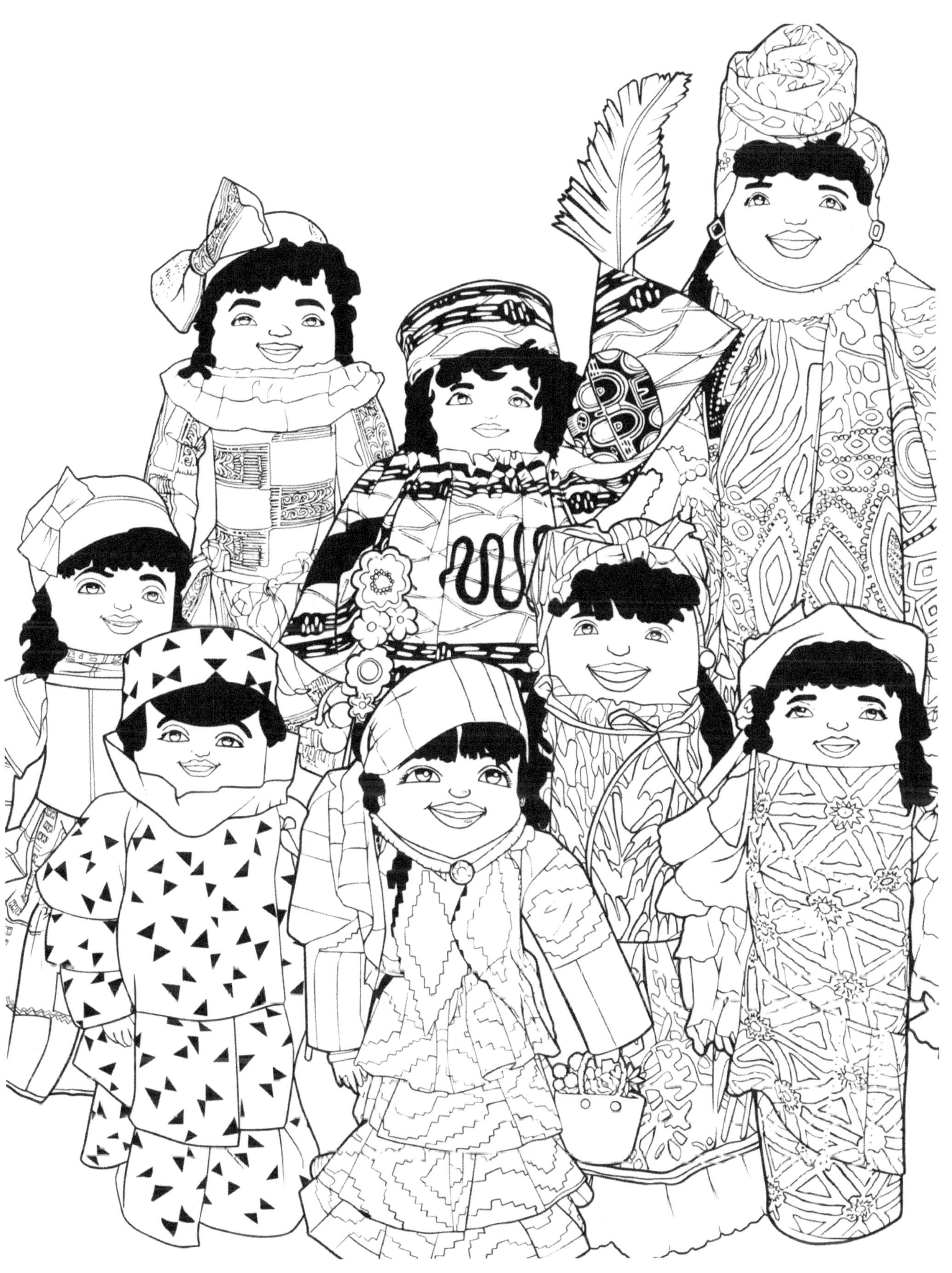

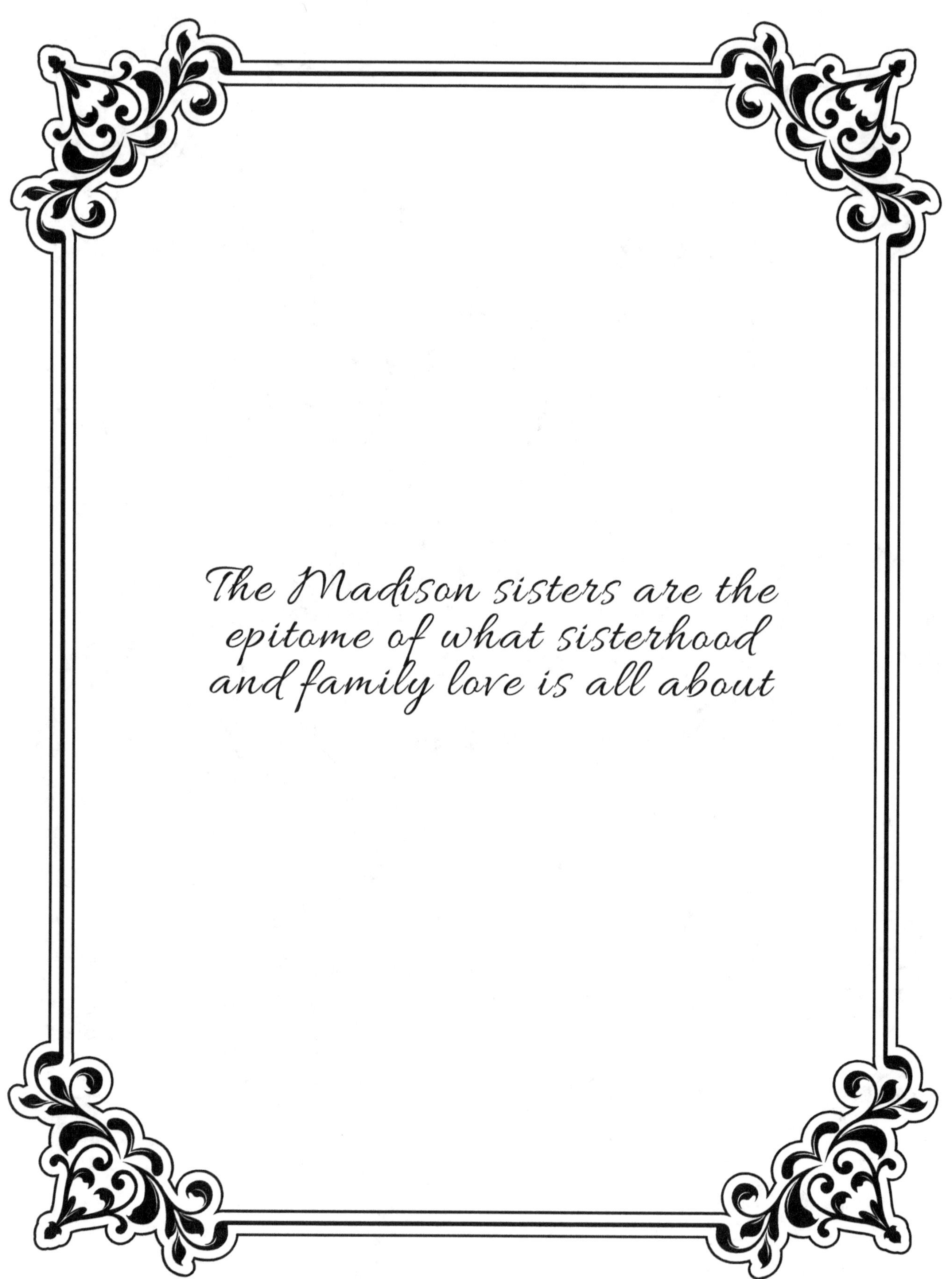

The Madison sisters are the epitome of what sisterhood and family love is all about

Luerine Madison Spencer

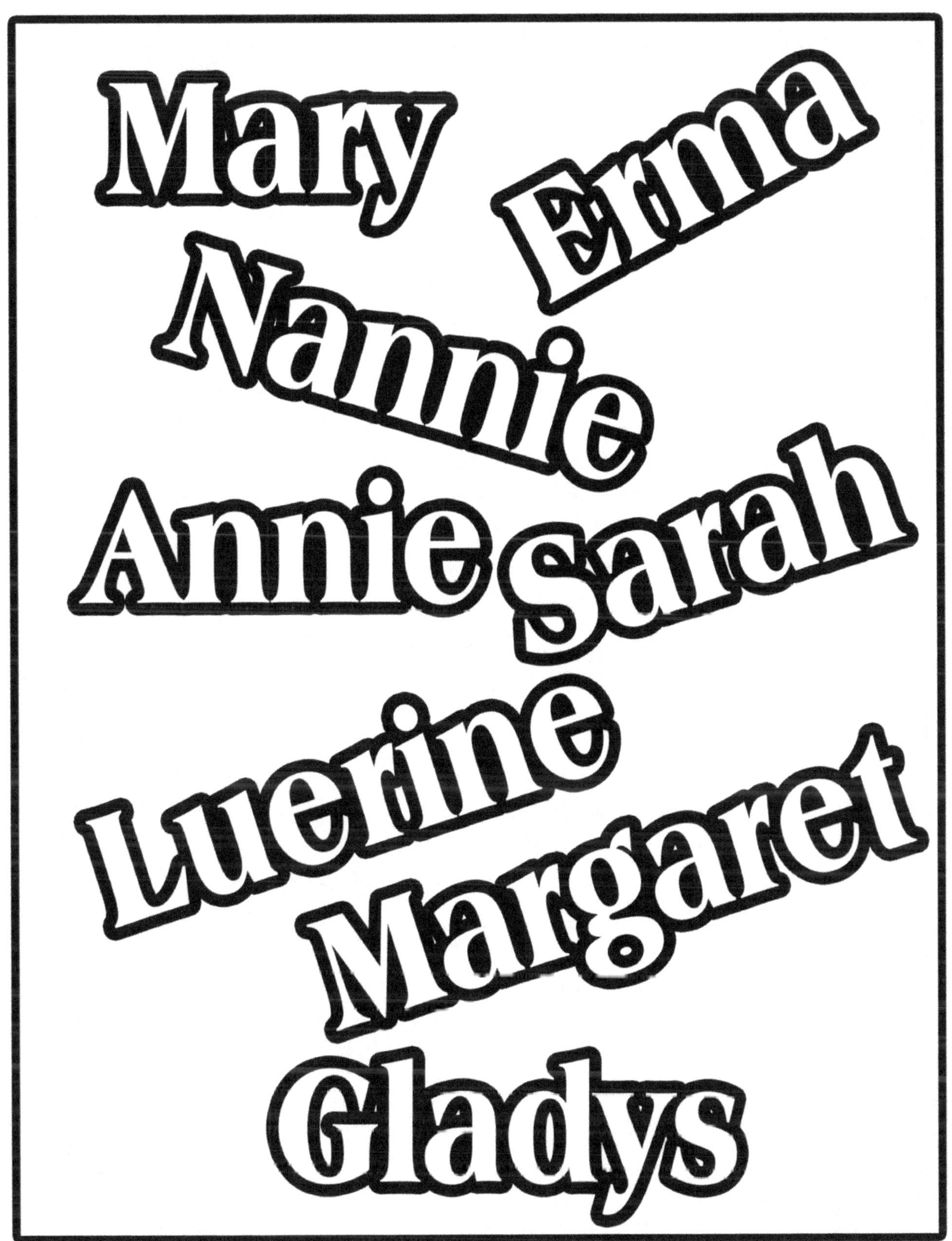

Mary
Erma
Nannie
Annie
Sarah
Luerine
Margaret
Gladys

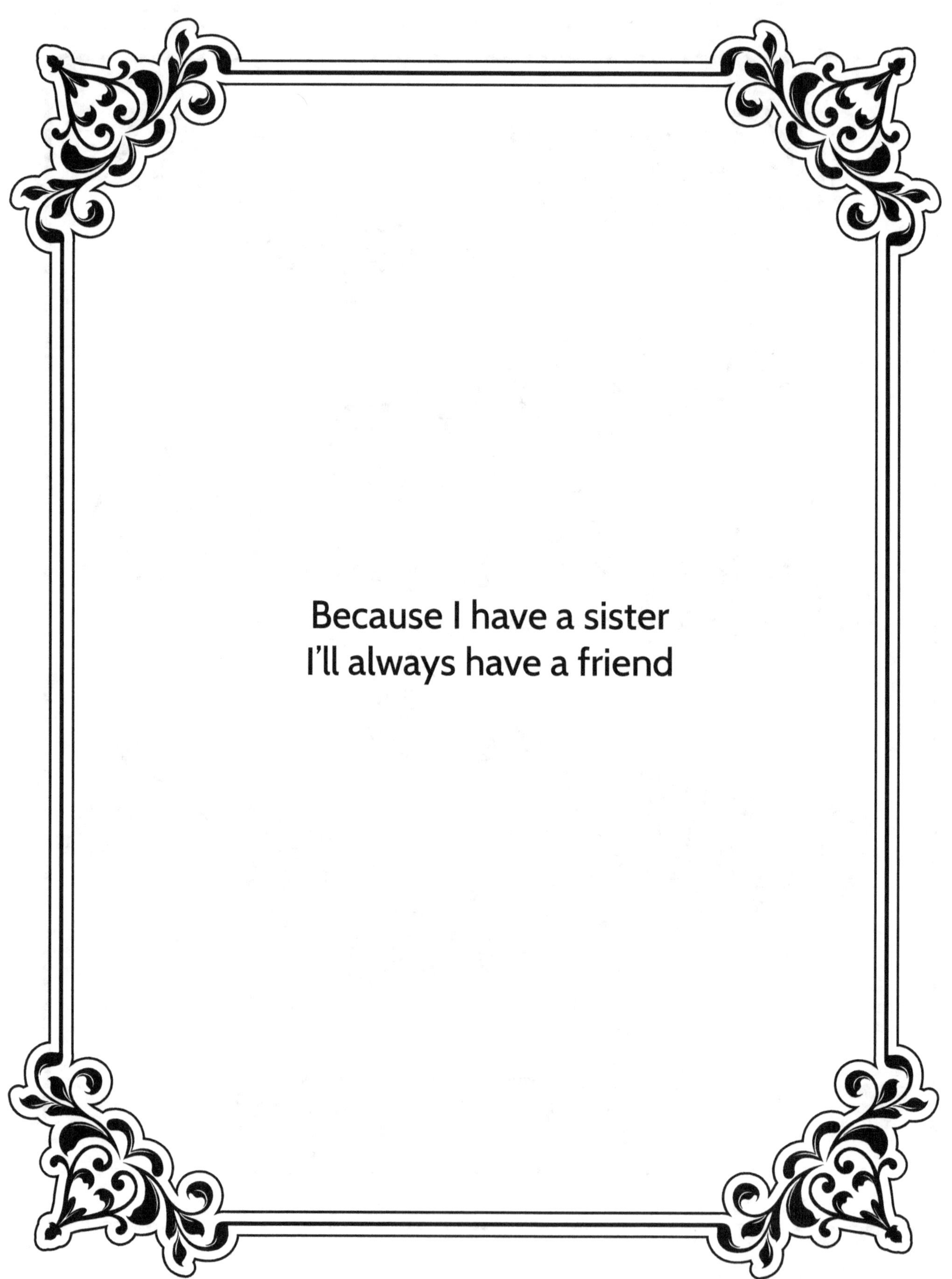
Because I have a sister
I'll always have a friend

Luerine Madison Spencer

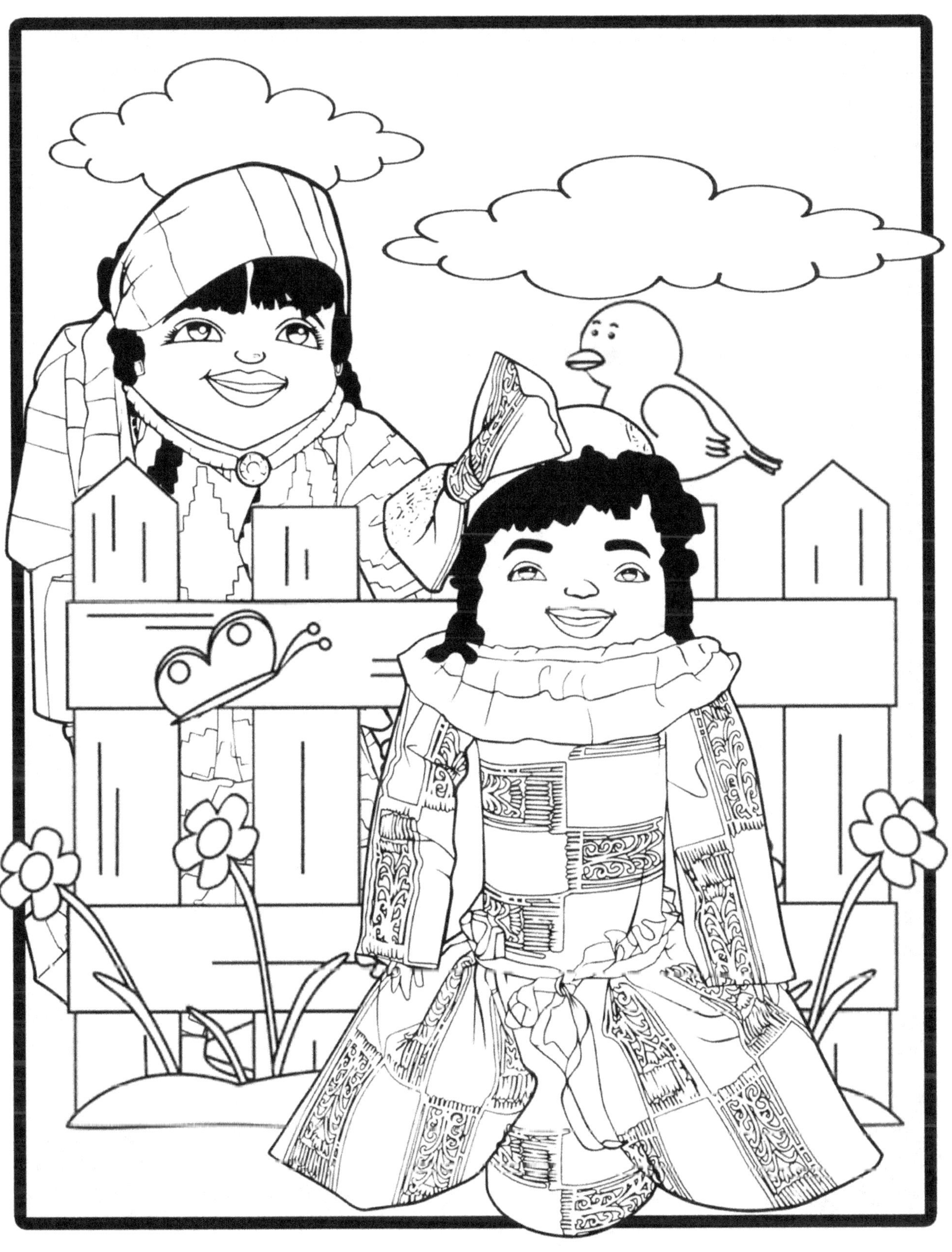

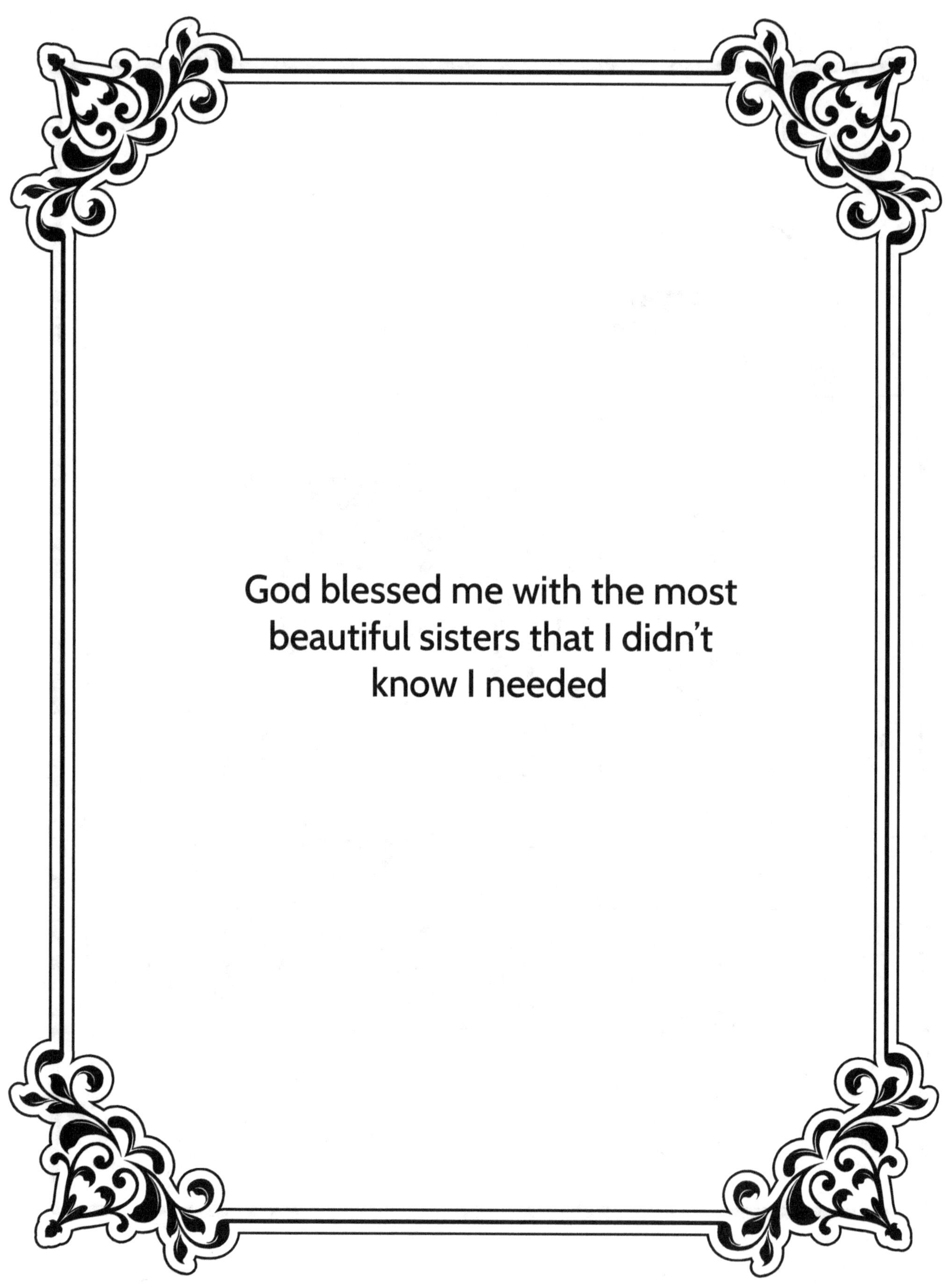
God blessed me with the most
beautiful sisters that I didn't
know I needed

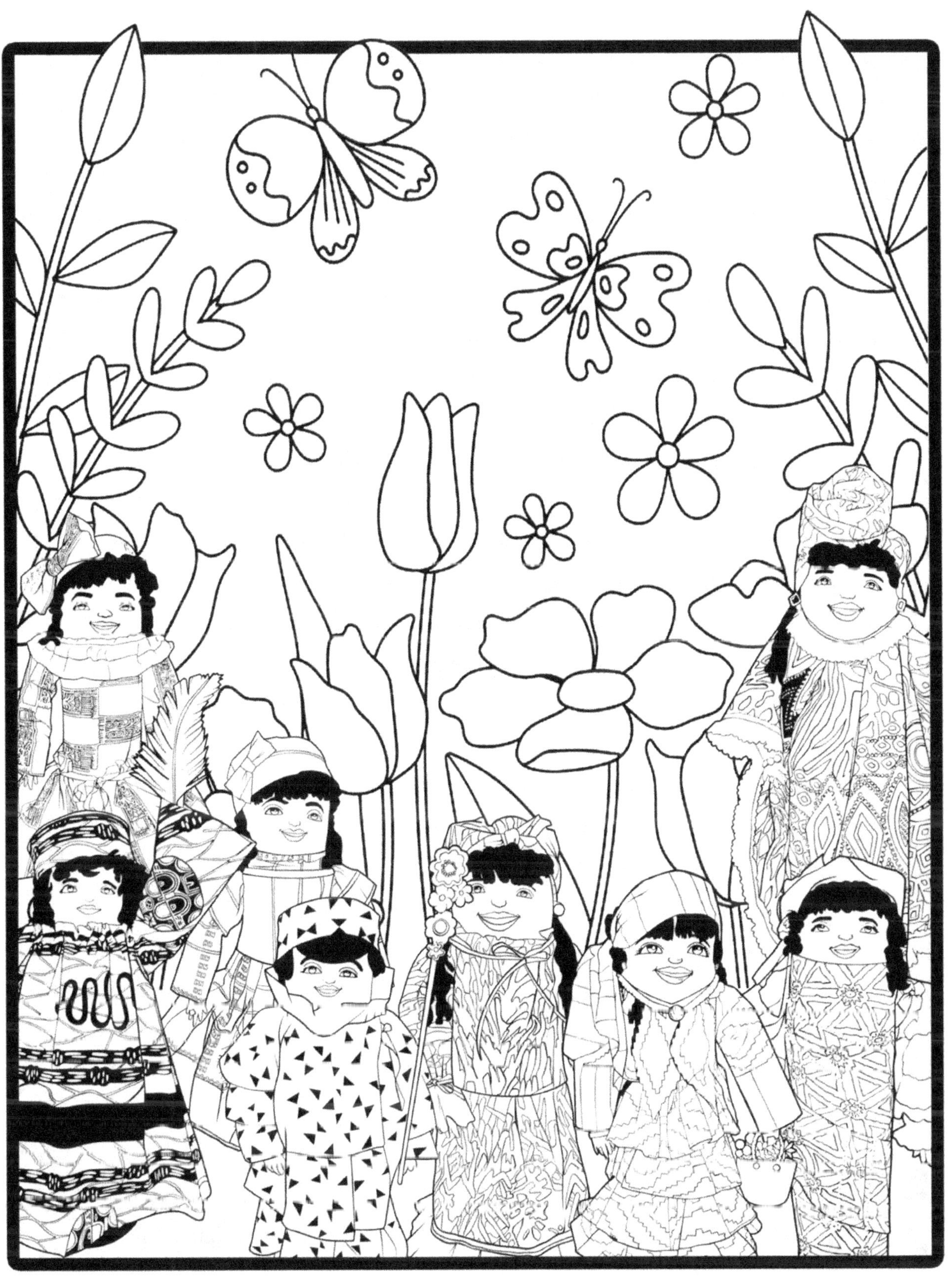

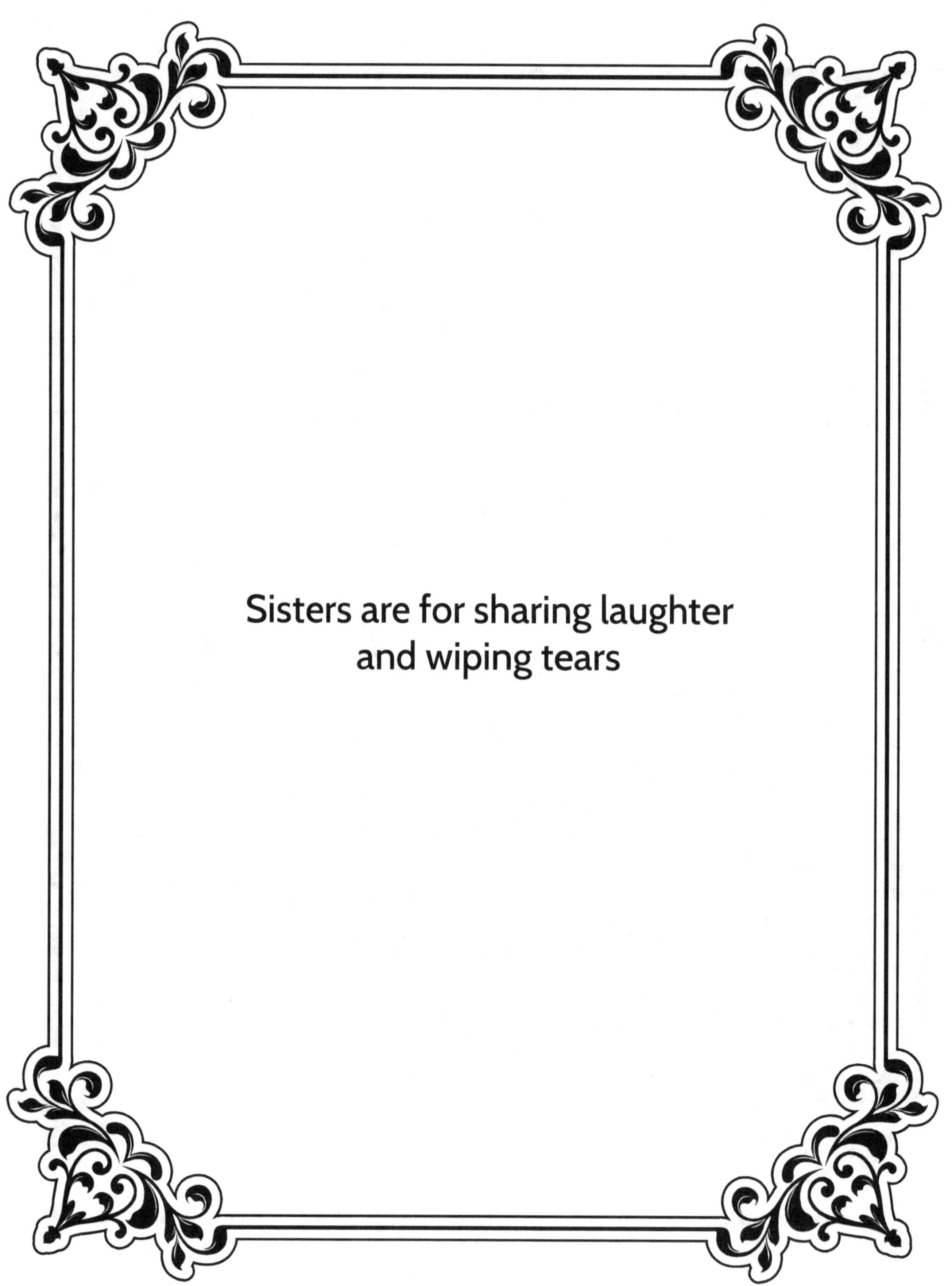
Sisters are for sharing laughter
and wiping tears

Luerine Madison Spencer

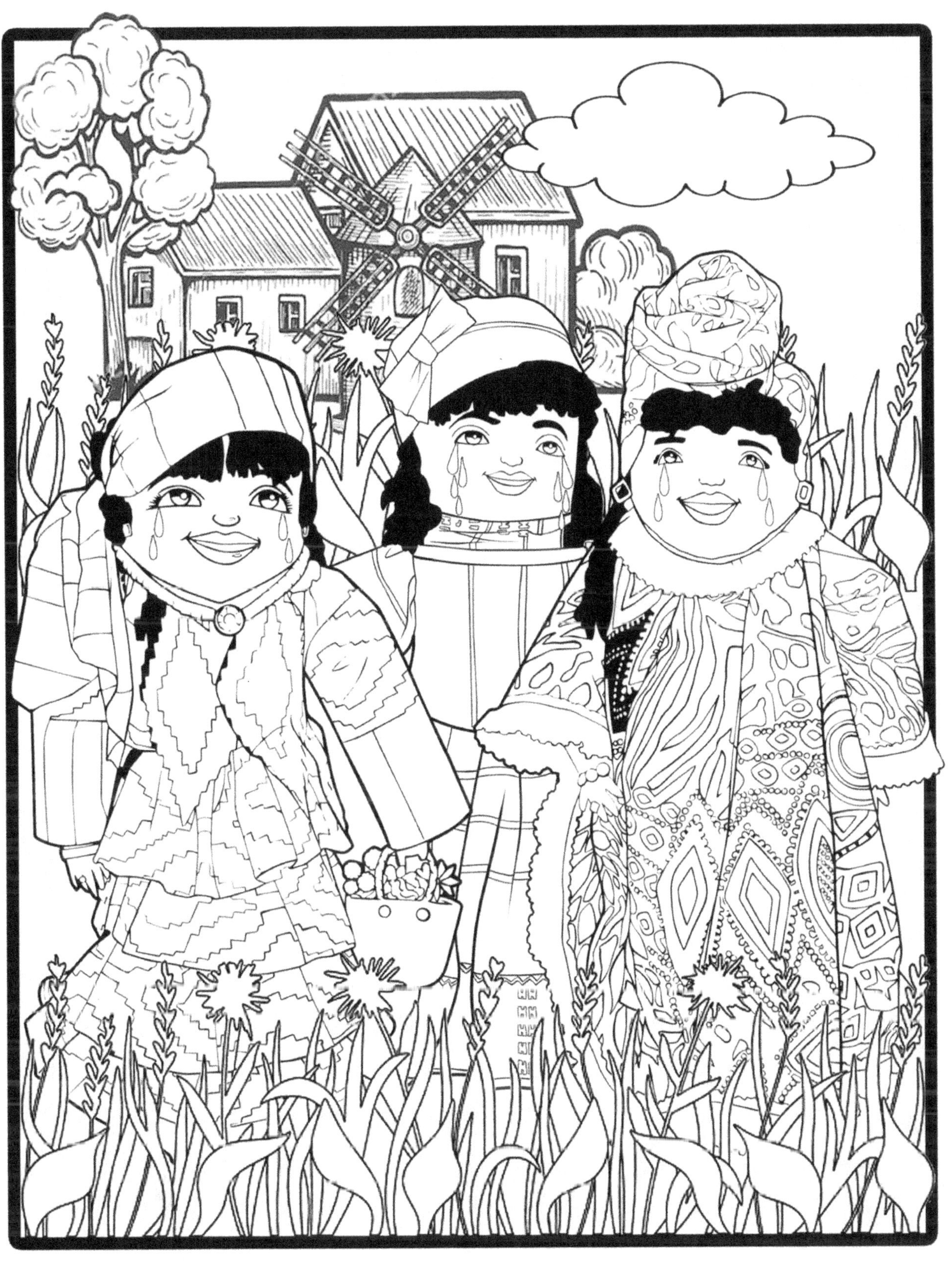

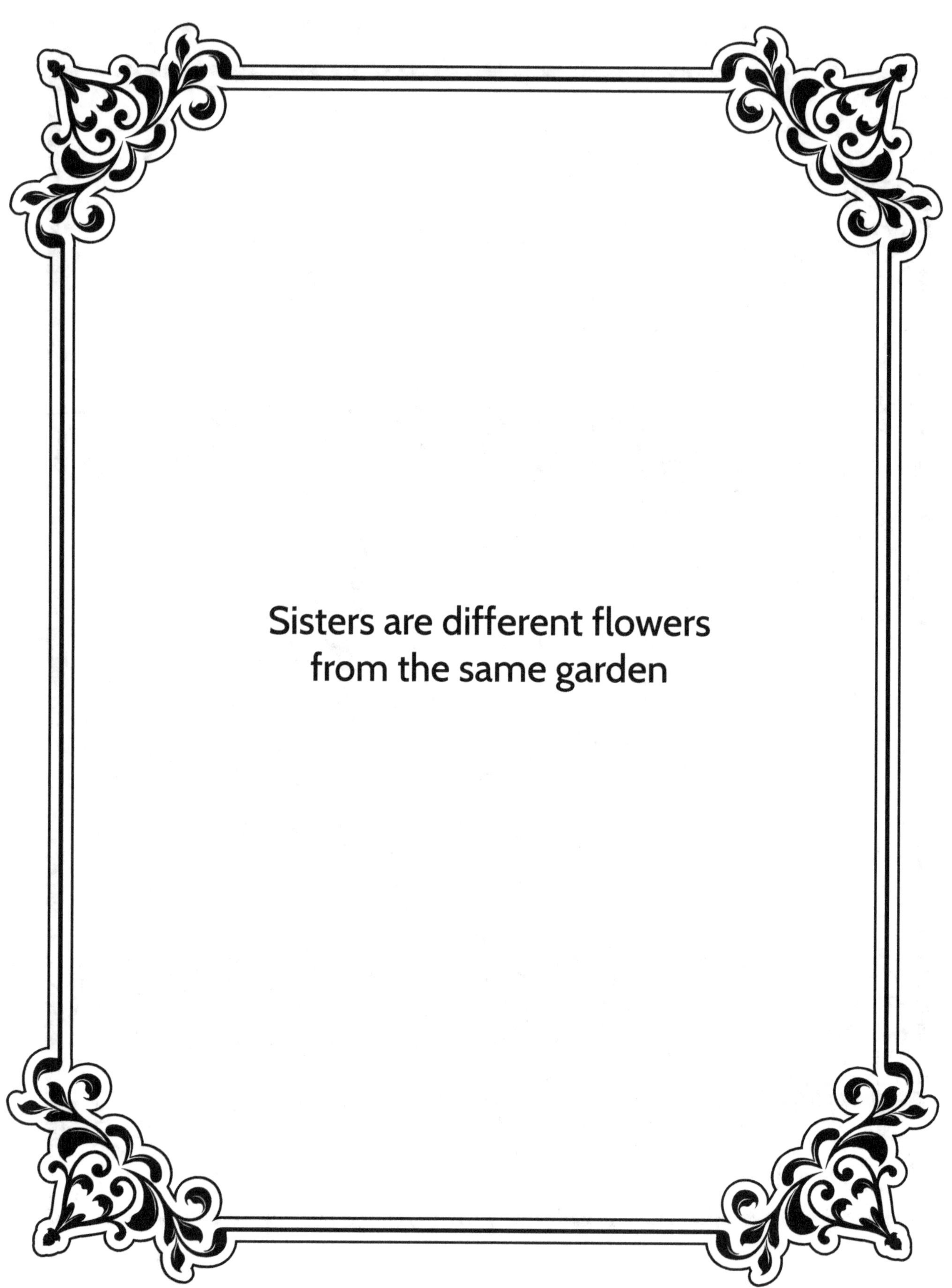
Sisters are different flowers
from the same garden

Luerine Madison Spencer

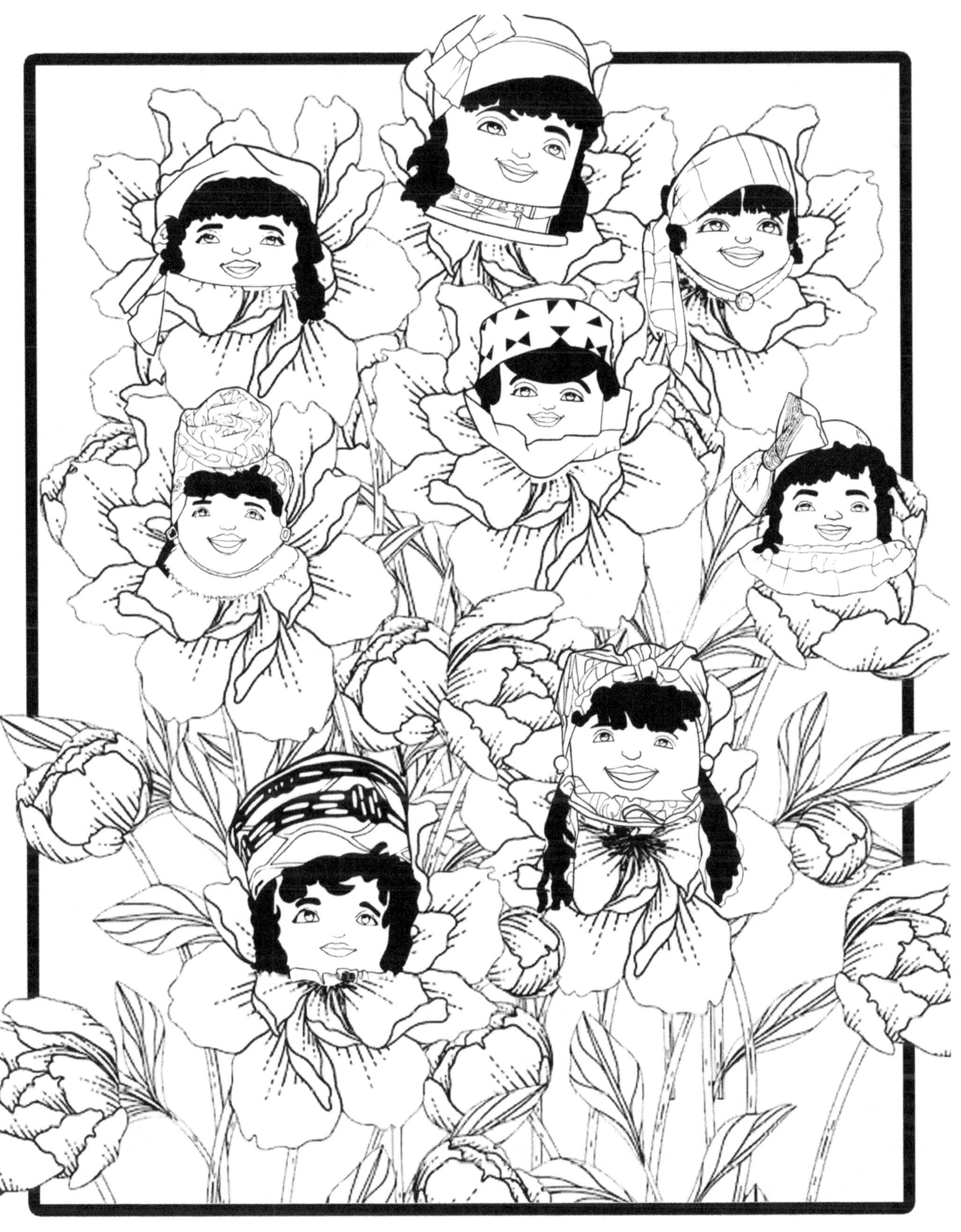

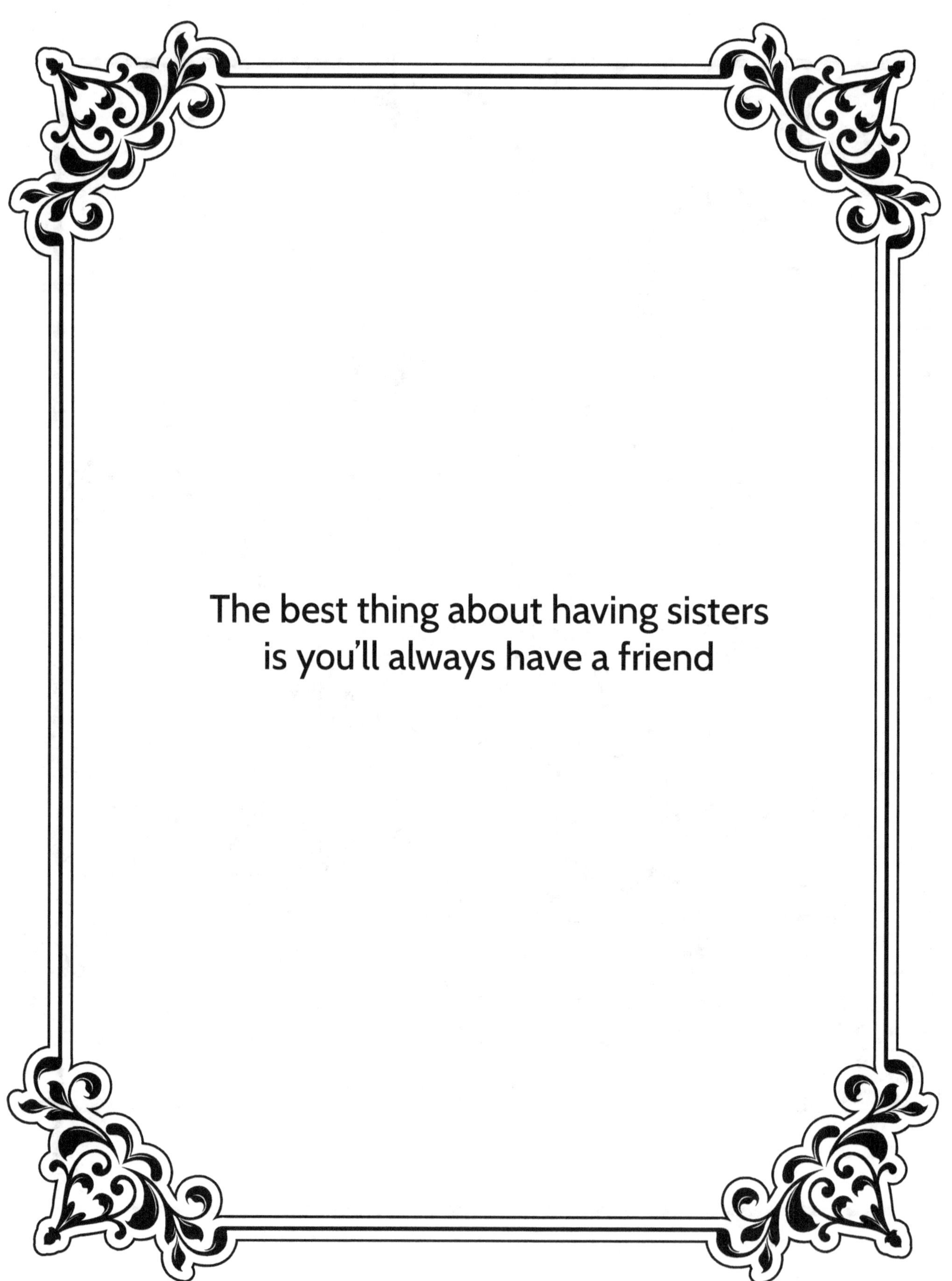
The best thing about having sisters
is you'll always have a friend

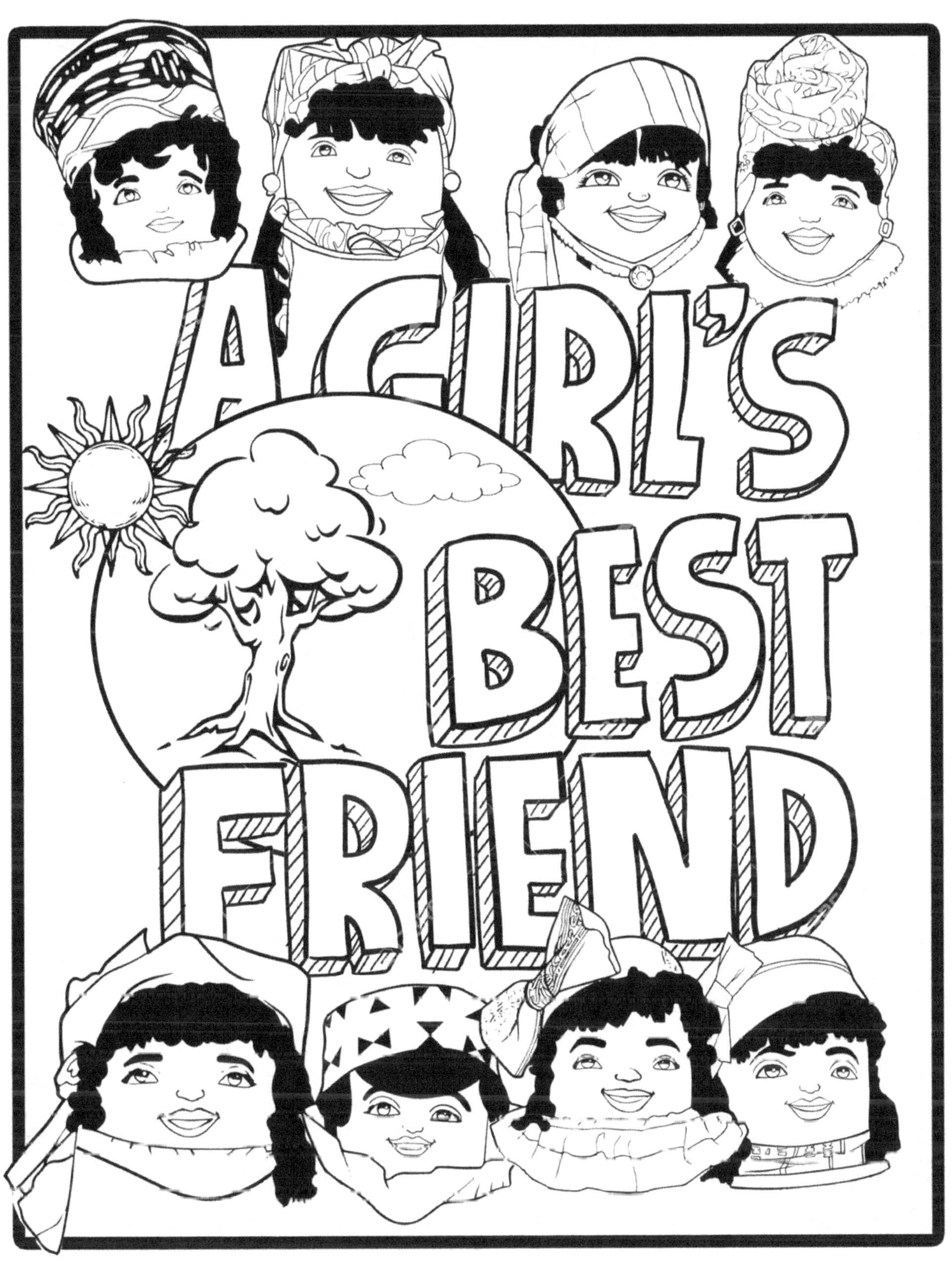
A GIRL'S
BEST
FRIEND

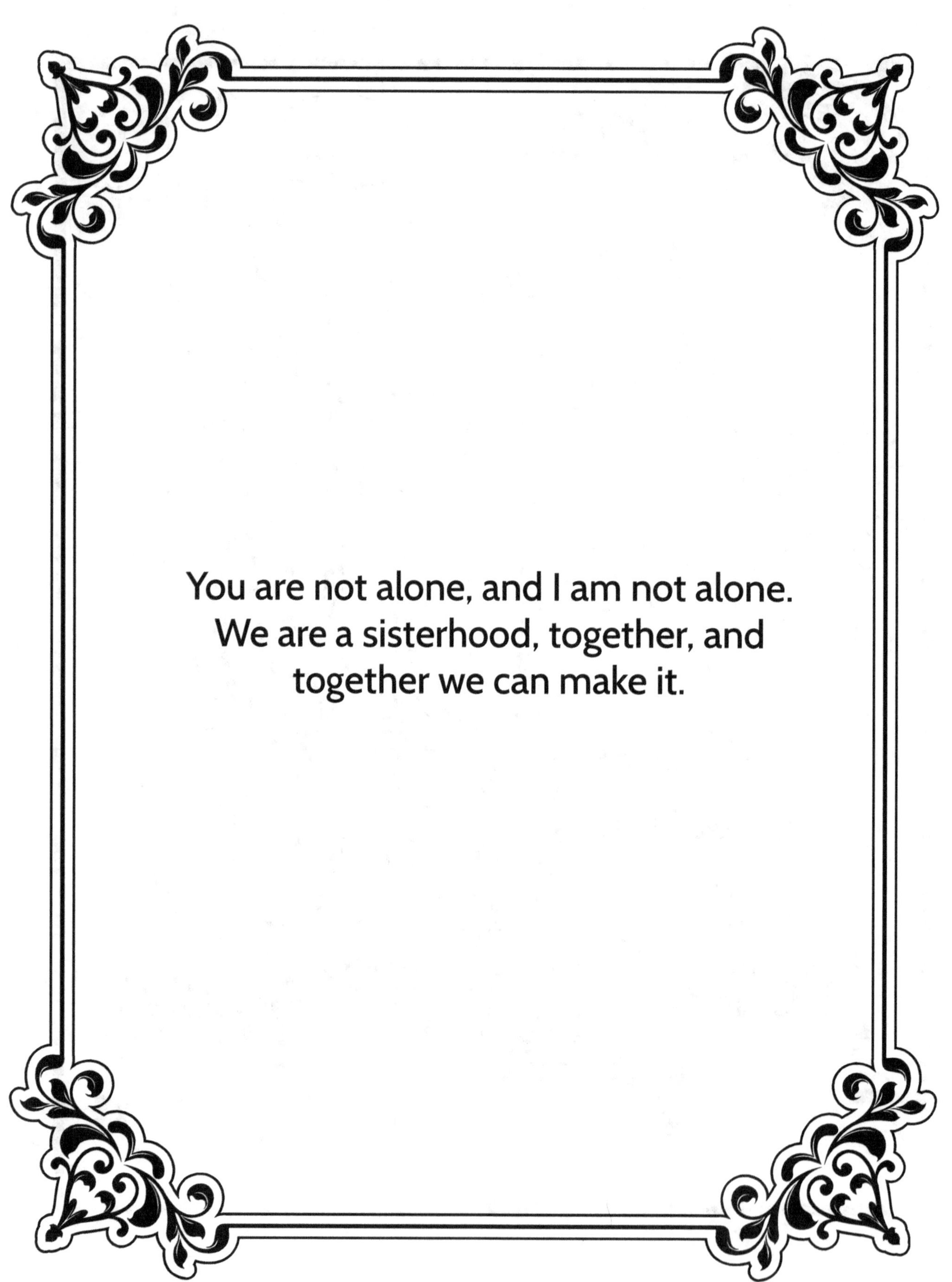

You are not alone, and I am not alone.
We are a sisterhood, together, and
together we can make it.

Luerine Madison Spencer

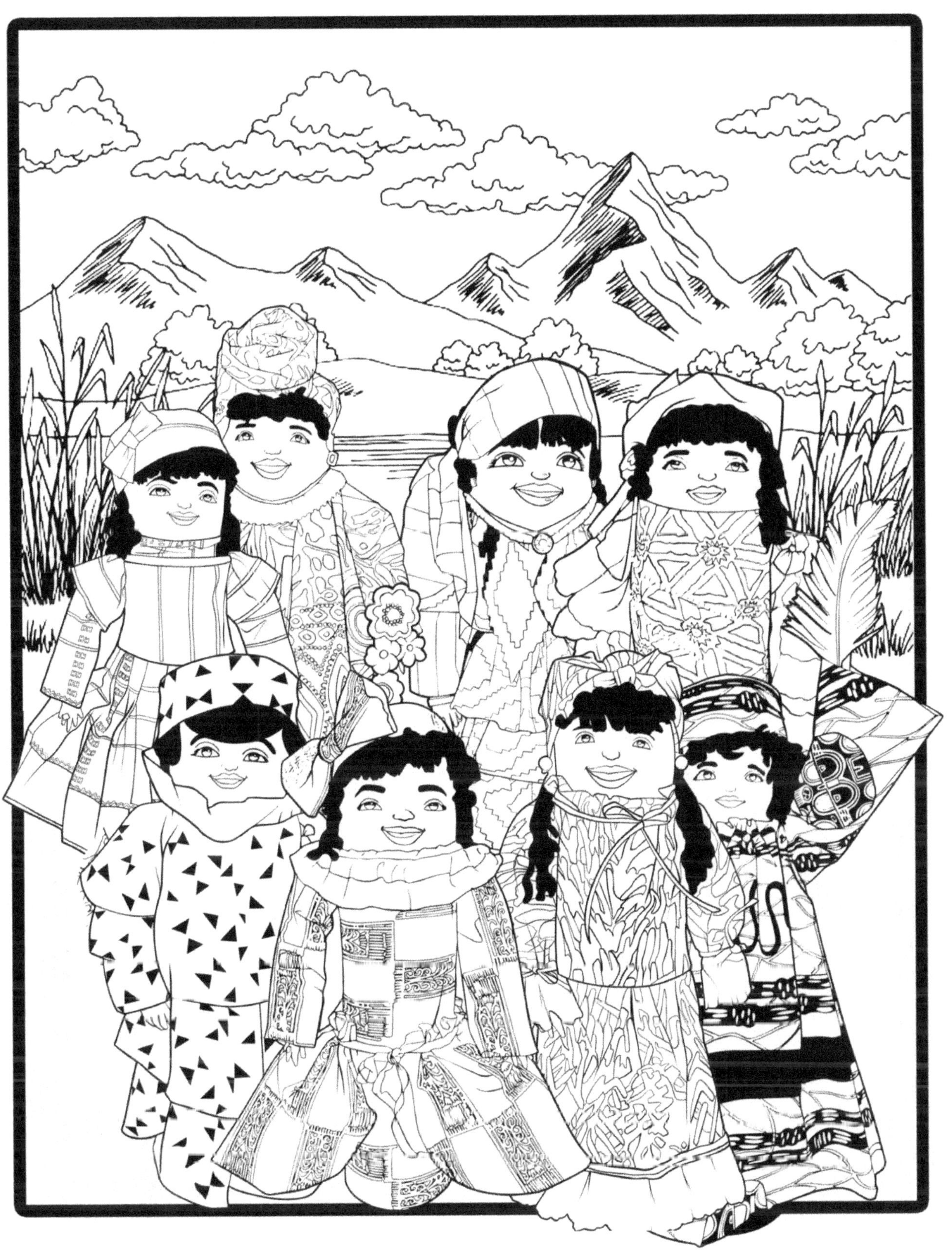

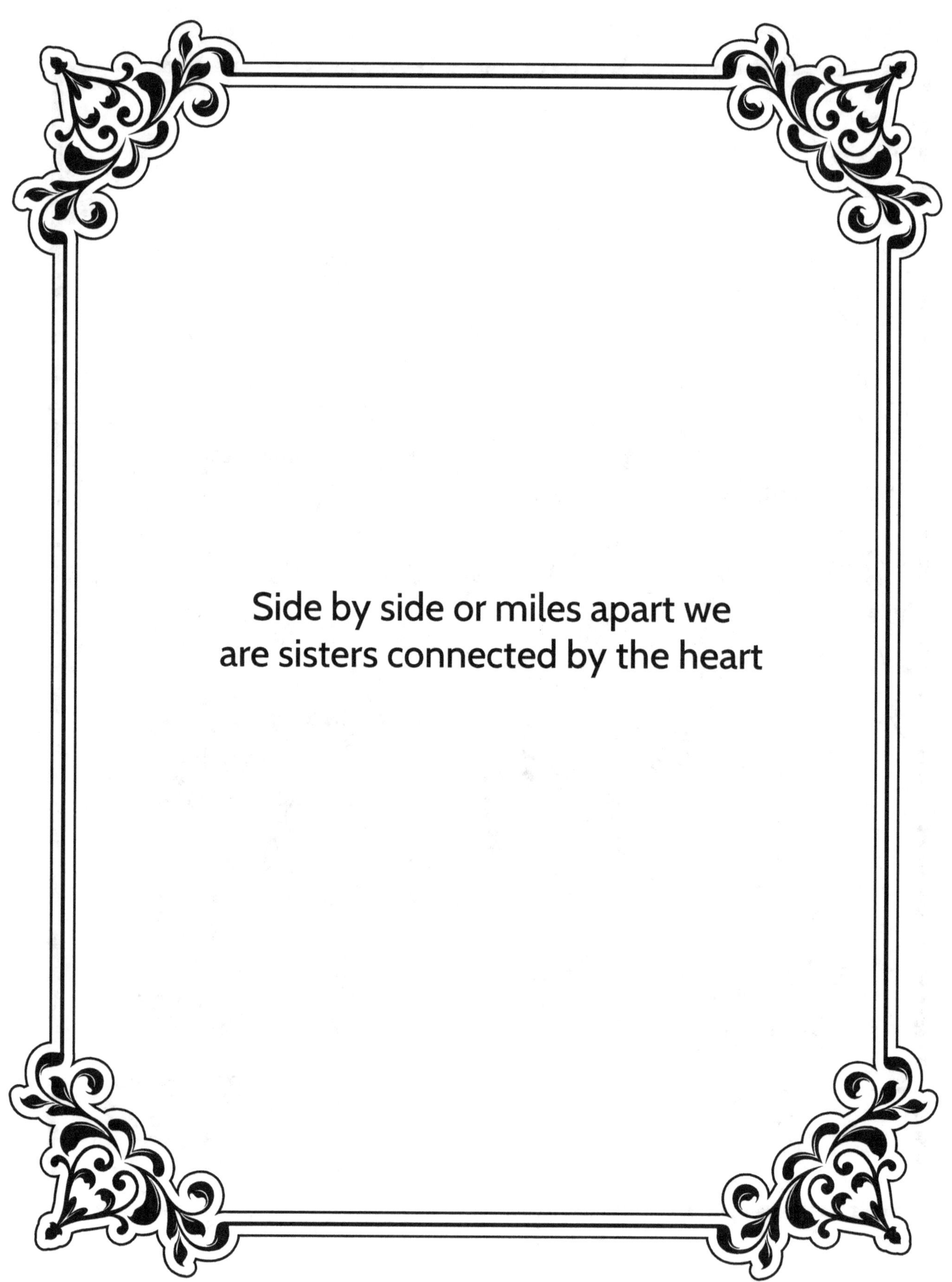

Side by side or miles apart we
are sisters connected by the heart

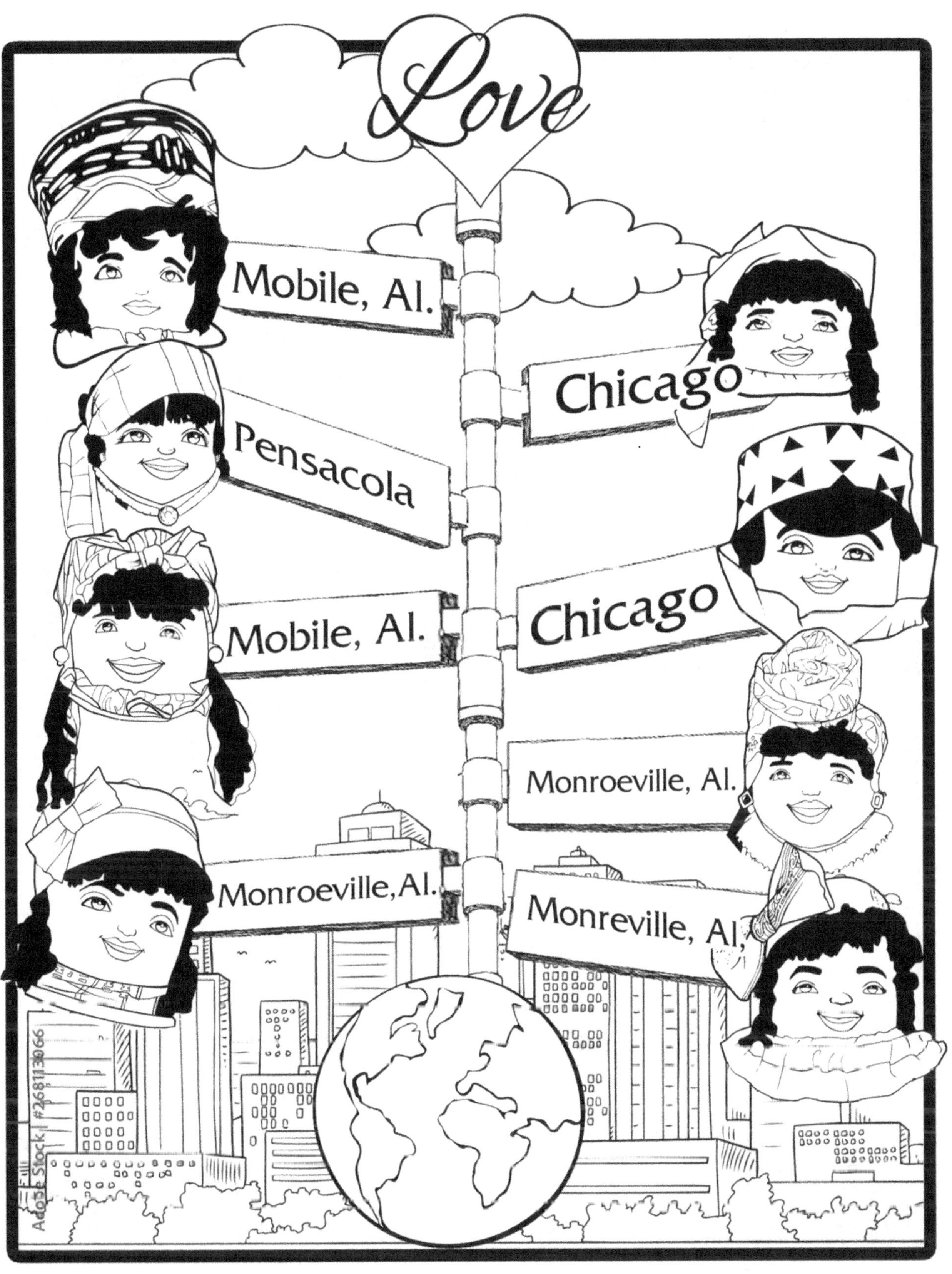
Love
Mobile, Al.
Pensacola
Mobile, Al.
Monroeville, Al.
Chicago
Chicago
Monroeville, Al.
Monreville, Al.
Adobe Stock #268113066

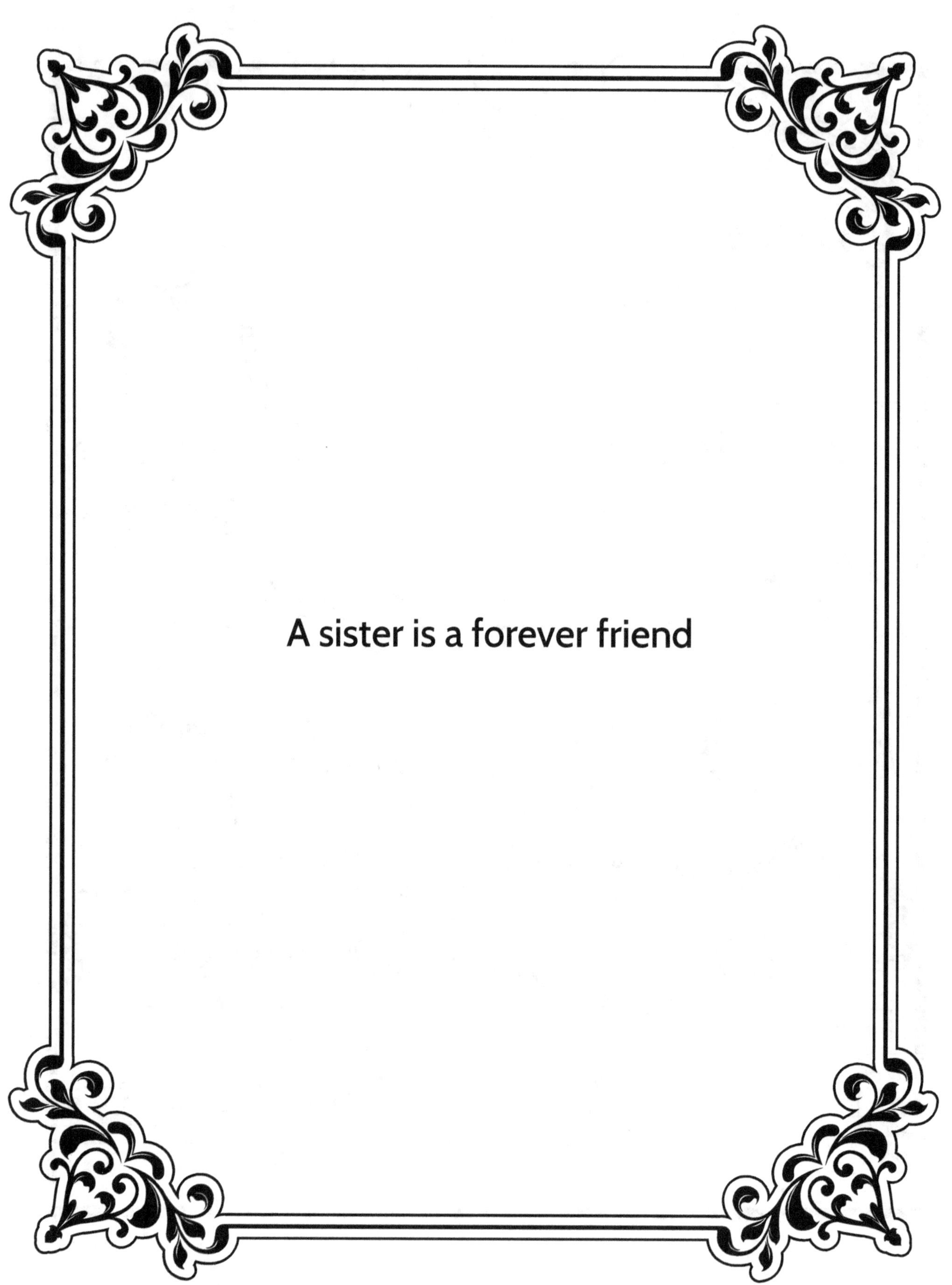

A sister is a forever friend

Luerine Madison Spencer

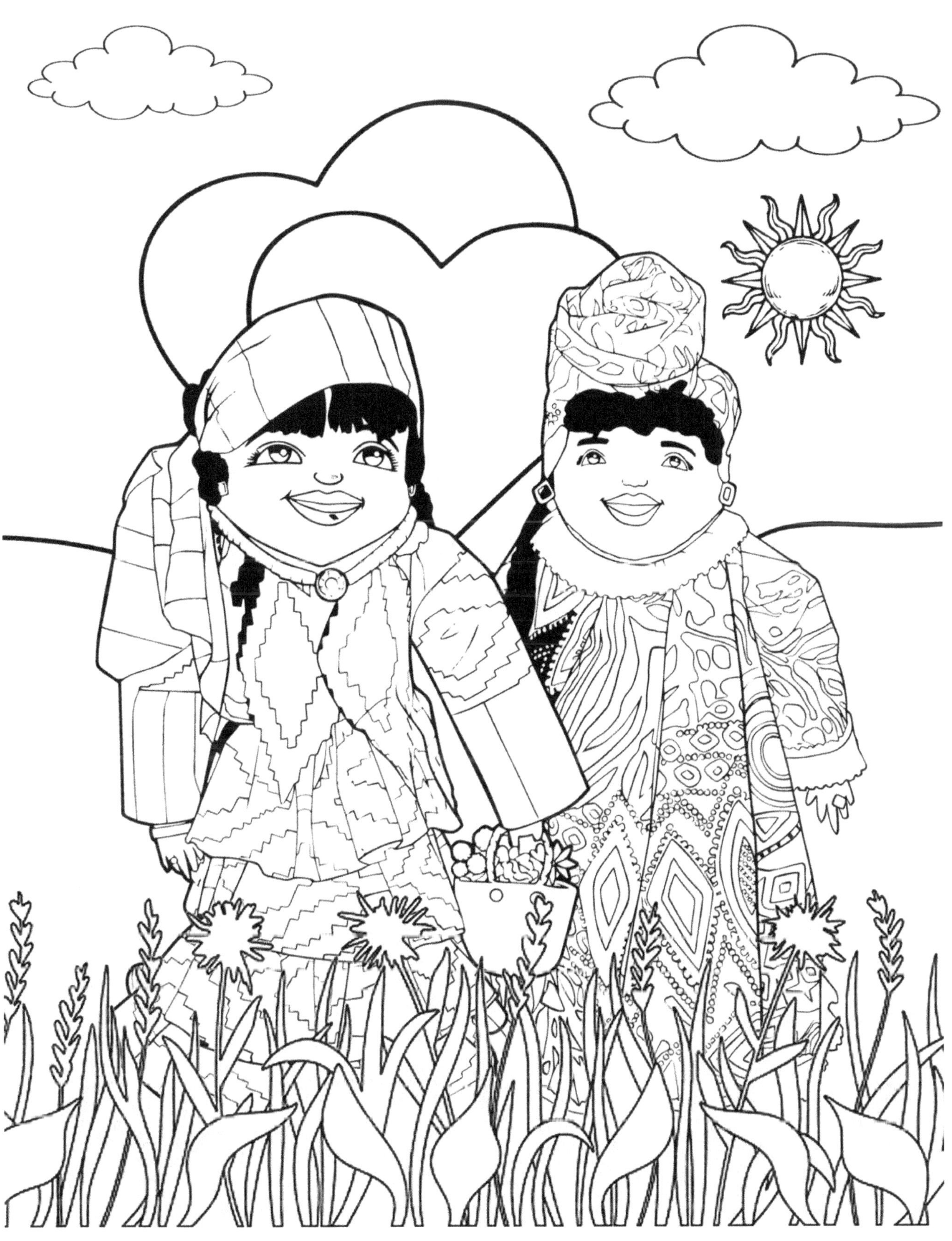

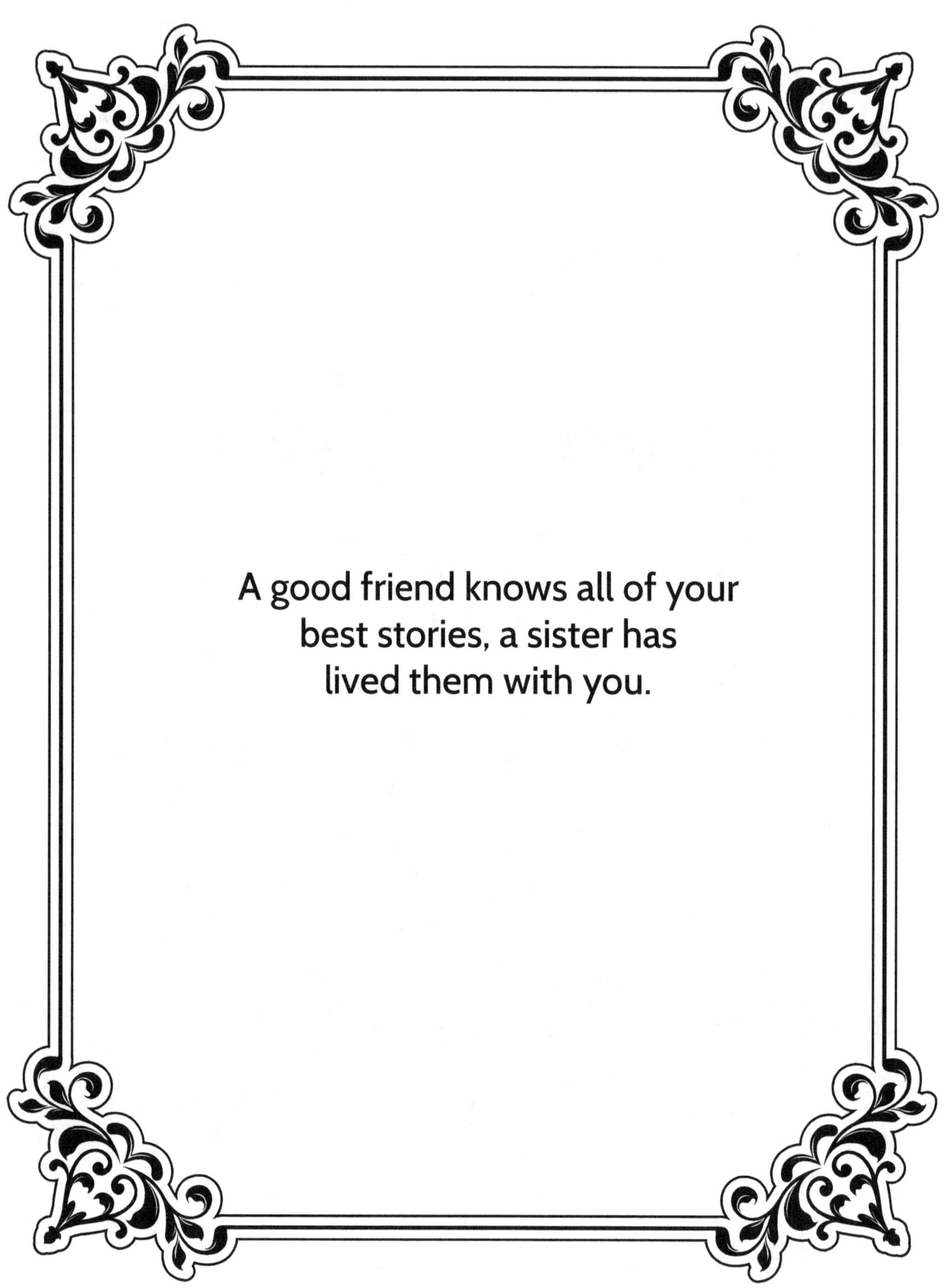
A good friend knows all of your
best stories, a sister has
lived them with you.

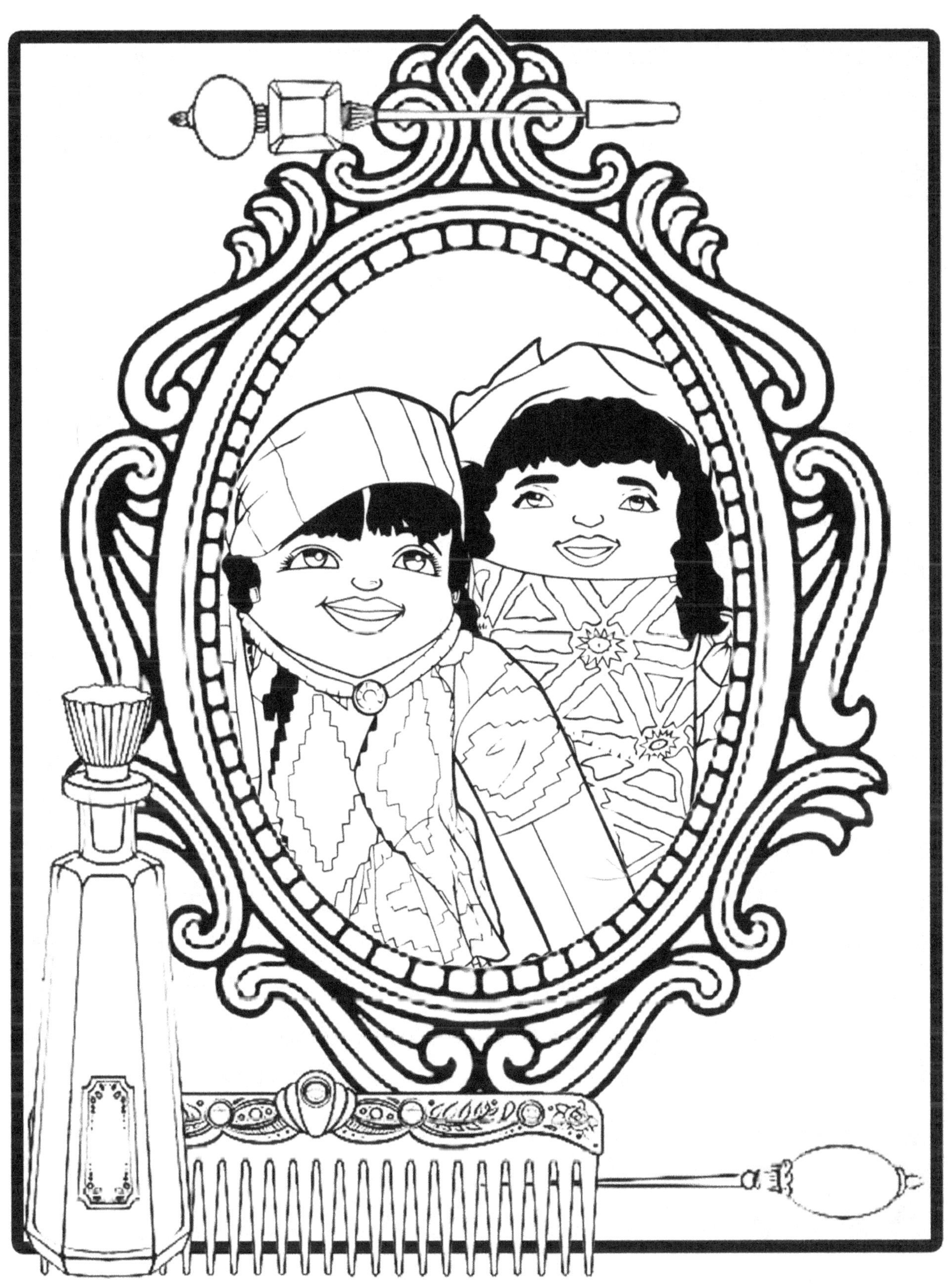

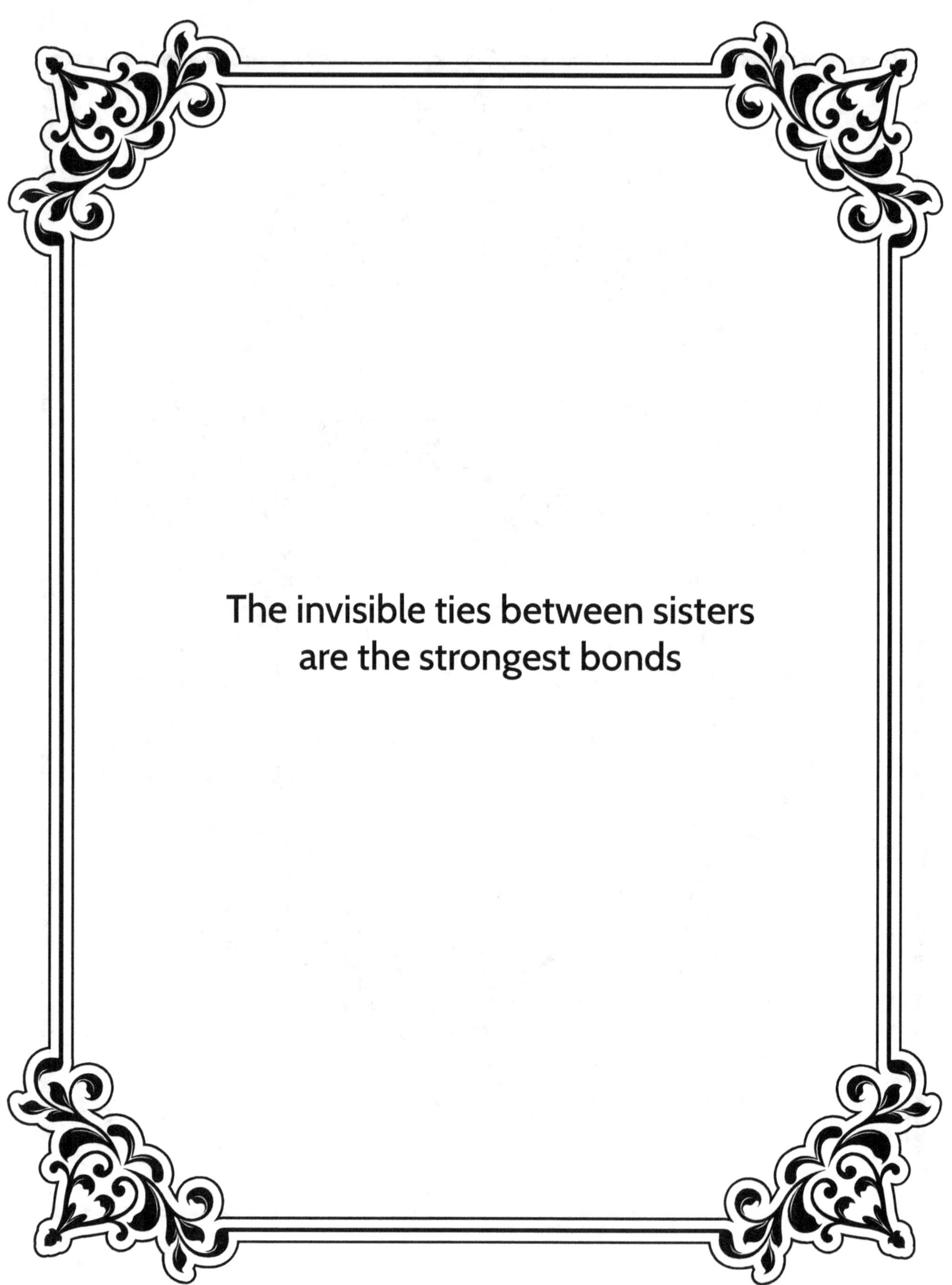
The invisible ties between sisters
are the strongest bonds

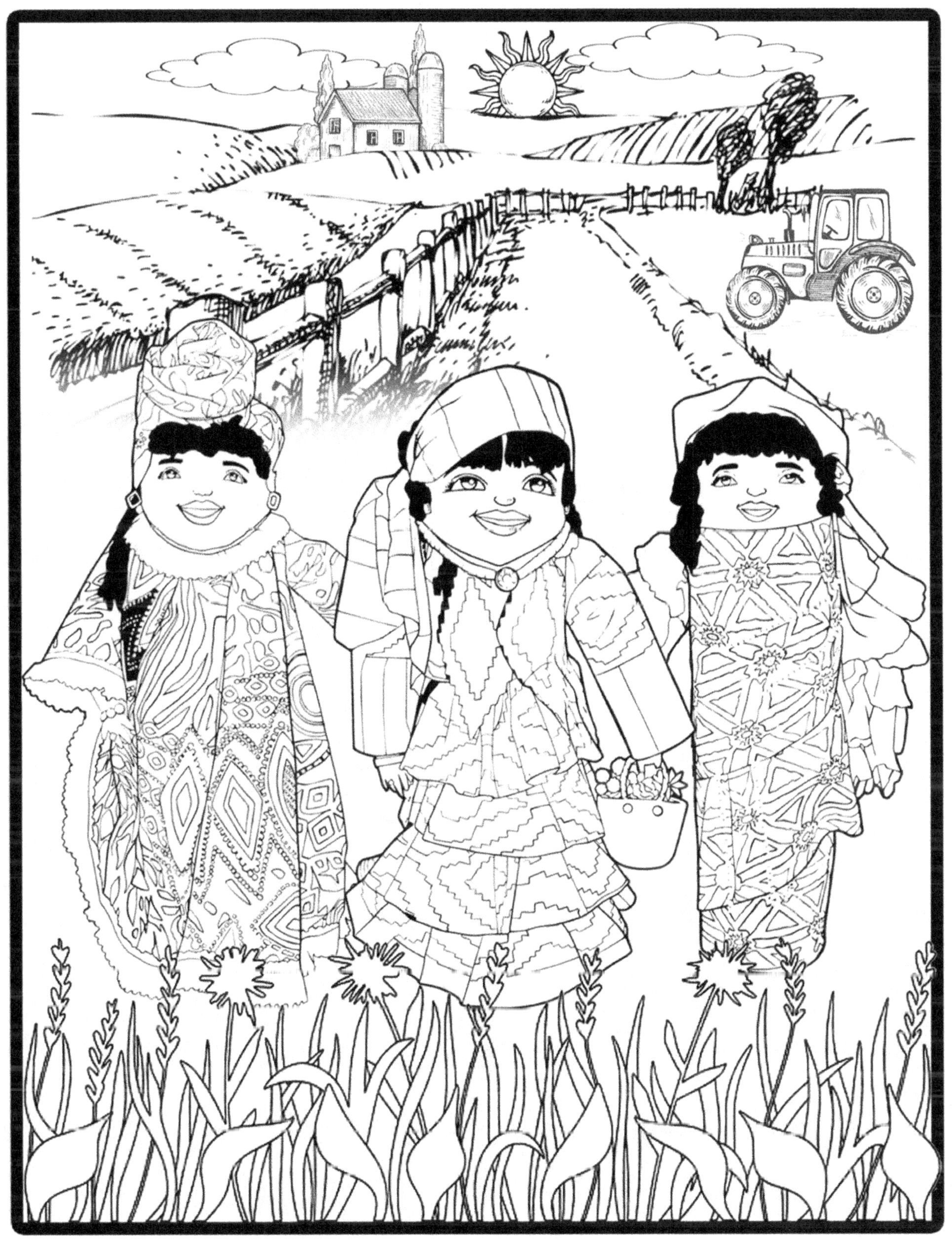

The Joy of Sisterhood

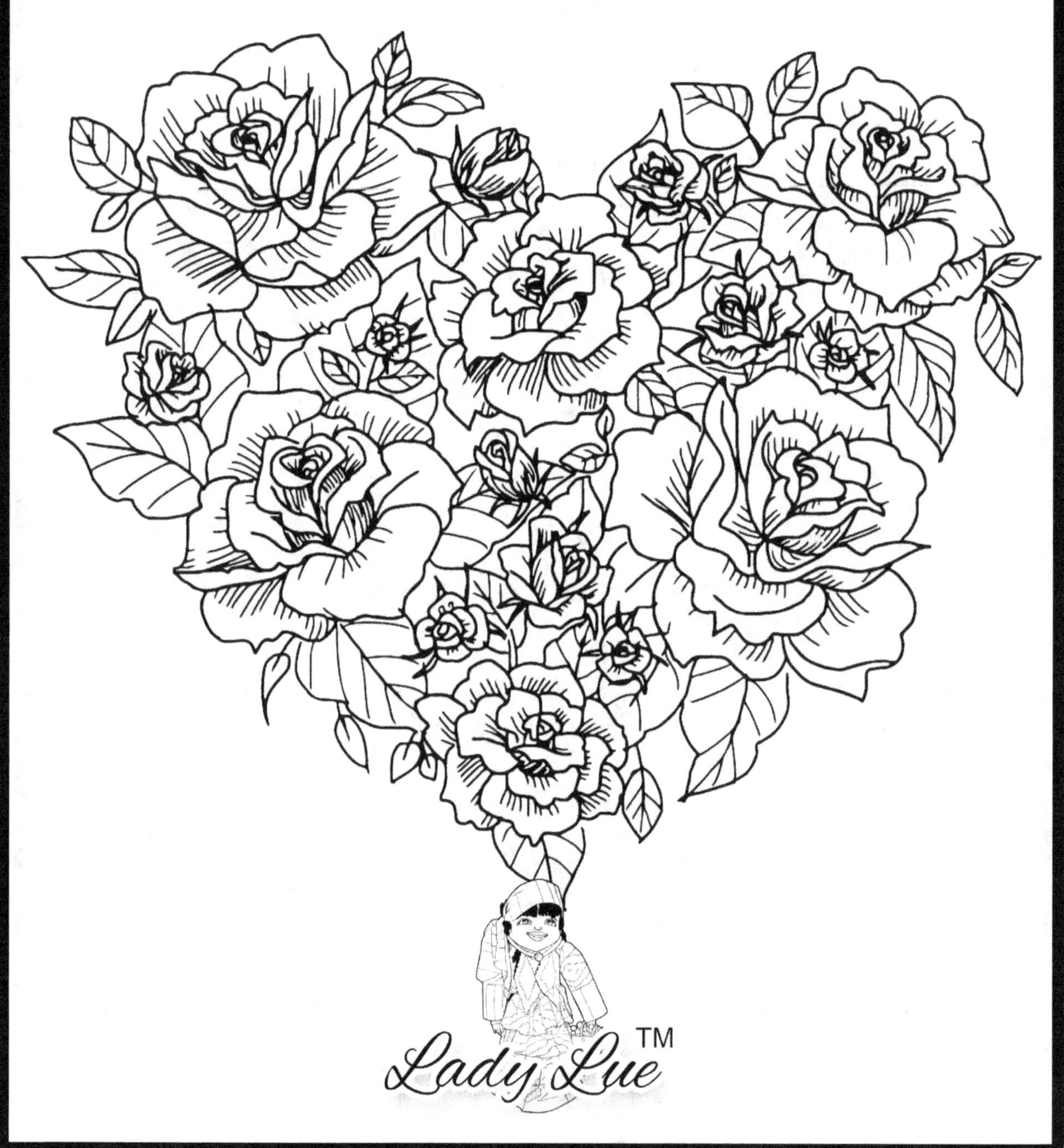